# The
# Education
# Dissertation

# The
# Education
# Dissertation

## A Guide for Practitioner Scholars

# Dan W. Butin

**CORWIN**
A SAGE Company

*For information:*

Corwin
A SAGE Company
2455 Teller Road
Thousand Oaks, California 91320
(800) 233-9936
Fax: (800) 417-2466
www.corwinpress.com

SAGE Ltd.
1 Oliver's Yard
55 City Road
London EC1Y 1SP
United Kingdom

SAGE India Pvt. Ltd.
B 1/I 1 Mohan Cooperative
    Industrial Area
Mathura Road, New Delhi 110 044
India

SAGE Asia-Pacific Pte. Ltd.
33 Pekin Street #02-01
Far East Square
Singapore 048763

Printed in the United States of America

*Library of Congress Cataloging-in-Publication Data*

Butin, Dan W. (Dan Wernaa)
The education dissertation: a guide for practitioner scholars/Dan W. Butin.
    p. cm.
Includes bibliographical references and index.
ISBN 978-1-4129-6043-4 (cloth: alk. paper)
ISBN 978-1-4129-6044-1 (pbk.; alk. paper)
    1. Dissertations, Academic—Authorship. 2. Academic writing. 3. Doctoral students—Psychology. I. Title.

LB2369.B87 2010
378.2'42—dc22                            2009023358

This book is printed on acid-free paper.

15  16  17  10 9 8 7 6 5

| | |
|---|---|
| *Acquisitions Editor:* | Debra Stollenwerk |
| *Associate Editor:* | Julie McNall |
| *Production Editor:* | Amy Schroller |
| *Copy Editor:* | Gretchen Treadwell |
| *Typesetter:* | C&M Digitals (P) Ltd. |
| *Proofreader:* | Wendy Jo Dymond |
| *Indexer:* | Judy Hunt |
| *Cover Designer:* | Scott Van Atta |

# *Contents*

# List of Figures

# *Preface*

C an I do it? This is the question I am consistently asked by experienced educators—teachers, principals, and central administrators—with years of success in the classroom and in leadership positions. Can I really complete the dissertation? This question may sound strange coming from individuals who are accomplished practitioners. Yet, they have all heard stories of students languishing for years pursuing research that is never completed; they have seen colleagues frustrated by the lack of support; they themselves have little patience for seemingly technical and abstract "academic" writing that has little relevance to their day-to-day professional lives.

But, I say to them, that is the wrong question. The right question is, How do I begin? Writing a dissertation is, of course, not easy. It may take many years and require immense focus and commitment. And, of course, one must have a passion, something about which one cares about, and a willingness to completely and deeply focus the dissertation research on this passion. With the requisite skills, passion, and dedication, then, an individual can indeed write a quality dissertation. Moreover, I say to these educators, the education community desperately needs more individuals capable of linking theory and practice. Such applied or "translational" research is crucial for improving education practices and policies; and yet, it is so difficult to do well. We need more practitioner scholars—educators able to bridge the divide between academic research and daily practice—who can bring ideas to life and research to fruition in their classrooms, school buildings, and districts.

The problem, as educational research and national data inform us, is that more than half of all doctoral students never complete their dissertations. For those that do, the average time for completion is over a decade. Doctoral programs and advisors may spend a lot of time on the explicit aspects of doctoral study—for example, the content of coursework, the importance of a solid research design—but there is usually very little guidance about the implicit and oftentimes most important part: how do I actually make it through this process? "How do I begin?"

is, thus, the key insight of this book. Specifically, I have written this book to show the step-by-step process in developing and completing a quality dissertation in a time-efficient manner.

## WHO SHOULD READ THIS BOOK AND WHY

This book is meant precisely for those individuals who have the passion and commitment to write a dissertation. Ideally, it is for students just beginning their doctoral studies or dissertation work. But, it can support students (and their advisors) at any stage of the dissertation process because it serves as a scaffolding—the strong support mechanisms—to complete an education dissertation in a timely and academically rigorous fashion. This book is grounded in adult-learning theory presuming that adult students are engaged learners who bring a wealth of experience and knowledge to their studies and, in turn, simply need a structured context to demonstrate and transfer their skills. This book, as such, provides the "big-picture" framework and the nitty-gritty details.

Doctoral students may have taken numerous research and theory courses; dissertation advisors may be experts in their fields. Yet, all too often, neither students nor faculty usually address the salient aspects of actually doing one's dissertation: How do I frame the research question? How do I begin a literature review? And when do I end it? Why do I have to use APA style? What's the point of a theoretical framework? What exactly does a dissertation chair do? And when do I go to her for help? It is not that doctoral students are incapable of asking or doctoral faculty unwilling to answer such questions. It is that we only rarely make explicit and systematize the tacit knowledge of writing a dissertation. This is exactly what this book offers: supporting the student–advisor relationship through the numerous stages and hurdles of the dissertation.

The dissertation process, nevertheless, is all too often presumed and expected to be a bumpy ride, as if the months or years of detours along the hallways and byways of the academy are somehow badges of honor. The intellectual, emotional, and financial scars along the way are preferred to the seemingly only other option of "dumbing down" to accommodate those who cannot handle this journey. In other words, we all too often either provide too much latitude for our students (hoping that they will figure it out on their own) or believe that we have to "babysit" our doctoral students through each and every step (demeaning the academic integrity of the doctorate).

However, there is a third way. Namely, it is possible to provide perspectives, protocols, and guidelines for what to do at key stages in the dissertation process. This will facilitate both stage-specific strategies and the heuristics (the "rules of thumb") that foster a student's metacognition, allowing more independence the next time around.

A couple of years ago, a doctoral student from a local prestigious university came to me in tears because, for six months, her committee had given her minimal guidance and did not expect her to defend her dissertation proposal for another ten months. Yet, she had already done the hard work of thinking through her ideas. All she needed was a clear structure for how to articulate her research questions, think through the implications for her methodology, and then format her dissertation proposal to a standard and acceptable protocol. She needed six weeks of focused help, not two years of self-guided wandering.

This is what this book provides—conceptual models to clarify thinking and pragmatic tools to focus the writing. The book offers effective templates, and guidelines for avoiding the tangents that are ineffective. Put otherwise, this book helps practitioner scholars focus, and explicates the key features of how and why such a focus functions, all without compromising the academic quality of the work. In fact, it only strengths the academic quality of the work as it frees up time to focus on what is truly important: your dissertation research.

This book is not a cookie-cutter recipe for creating a dissertation "by the numbers." There is no such thing. (Or at least there shouldn't be.) A dissertation is an in-depth and rigorous examination of a particular issue that provides new knowledge and/or perspectives. As such, it contributes to ongoing scholarship and discussion around that issue. That can't be done for someone. Nor is this book a compilation of anecdotes and "war stories" about the journey ahead and seemingly sage advice for picturesque photo opportunities or places to avoid. While every dissertation is unique, every dissertation also has a highly formulaic academic structure. This book describes and details this structure in order to provide concrete and focused guidelines and guideposts at every stage of the dissertation process.

## KEY FEATURES AND HOW TO USE THEM

I have provided a host of strategies and features that will make the dissertation process much more effective. Specifically, I have created useful templates, synthesized key research, highlighted important milestones, and provided specific guiding activities and examples of student work. My overarching goal, above and beyond all of the known challenges to the dissertation process, is to shed light on and systematically overcome much of the uncertainty of the process. Doctoral students are often frustrated by the fact that there is so much that they do not know: What am I missing that everyone else seems to know about? What should I have asked that I did not even know to ask? Such "unasked questions"—the ones we don't even know to ask—are crucial to answer. I answer such questions at every stage of the dissertation process: What is a quality dissertation? What does my committee do? How long should chapters be? Is there a chance that I will fail my defense? Some of these questions do not have definitive answers, but they still must be explored. I do this in multiple ways.

## Organizational Templates

Organizing one's time and effort is crucial to success. I have provided templates to, among other things, organize a research timeline, structure the table of contents, and focus a literature review. These templates serve as heuristics that can be directly applied to, and modified for, a specific institution and research focus. I have listed these templates as figures in the table of contents so that they can be easily accessed and used; one can copy the page and personalize it for the specific context.

## Synthesis of Research

There is an immense amount of educational research on nearly every aspect of the dissertation process; it is difficult to know where to even begin. Therefore, I have focused on some the most important components—choosing a theoretical framework, developing a research design, and using the appropriate methodology—and provided suggestions for deeper investigation. In each chapter, I cite some of the key literature, and at the end of the book, I provide a list of key texts as additional resources.

## Key Milestones and Procedures

All too often, the dissertation process appears as an immensely abstract and distant goal. I have broken it down, step-by-step, and articulated the key milestones for each stage and how to most effectively obtain them. Whether this involves the Institutional Review Board (IRB) submission, aligning data and conclusions, or publishing dissertation research, I provide concrete goals and workable methods.

## "Hints" Along the Way

There are dozens of occasions in the dissertation process where we want to say, "Oh, by the way, I should have mentioned that . . ." I provide numerous "hints" throughout the book: How do I know when my topic is focused enough? What exactly is the role of a dissertation chair? How should I best prepare for my defense? These hints help students realize and think through situations that they may not even have realized they needed to know about. These are also listed in the table of contents for easy reference.

## Relevant Activities

It is critical that students understand important concepts—how to start a literature reviews correctly, how to focus research questions, and how to operationalize ideas. I provide specific activities at each stage of the process and list these activities in the table of contents to help students and faculty do these activities on their own or together in class.

## Examples of Student Work

We all have to start somewhere in developing our own research tools and organizing ideas; where we start greatly determines where we'll go and how fast we'll get there. That is why the first steps are so crucial and so difficult to make. I provide examples of student work throughout the book and analyze what was done well and what could have been modified or expanded. This allows the reader a chance to see helpful and workable examples, as well as realize the opportunities for modification to one's own studies and situations.

I provide such features and strategies throughout the book with the premise that the more one knows about each step and the more one understands how each protocol functions, the better one will move through this process. I thus suggest that you read this book from start to finish at the beginning of your doctoral program and continue to use it along the way. I want you to know where you are going before you begin because this will help you to think about each step in a much more conscious, clear, and coherent manner. You can, of course, return to specific sections of the book when you are at those stages in your own dissertation process. Additionally, many of the activities and templates are useful at multiple stages. The real key, though, is to understand your goals in order to focus your means.

So, when someone—a prospective applicant, a doctoral student stuck at the dissertation-proposal stage, or a faculty member editing a rough first draft of a dissertation—asks me whether or not he can do it, if it is actually possible to complete the dissertation, I don't simply encourage him to continue or just commiserate with his situation. I don't give abstract suggestions or anecdotal advice. Instead, I provide detailed and concrete suggestions, guidelines, and examples. I provide the big picture, a conceptual framework that clarifies how to think about this process. I have written this book to provide you with such support during this important stage in your career. I hope it is of help.

# *Acknowledgments*

**D**eb Stollenwerk, my editor at Corwin, was instrumental in bringing this book to fruition. From the moment I introduced her to the idea; through the weeks and months when she supported my revisions; to the, finally, last moments of production, Deb was conscientious in her guiding support, incisive in her feedback and suggestions, and wonderfully helpful in making this work truly professional. This book is a shining reflection of her skills. Likewise, Amy Schroller was instrumental in flawlessly guiding the production of the book, and Gretchen Treadwell's copyediting produced a truly crisp and flowing document. I am grateful to both of them for such work. Additionally, the anonymous reviewers provided wonderfully constructive feedback. I gained much from their comments and this book is much stronger from their input.

The doctoral faculty in the educational leadership program at Cambridge College have pushed my thinking on all aspects of this book: Sandy Bridwell, Jim Horn, Kathleen Lynch, Steve Maio, Fernando Padro, and Kemoh Salia-Bao. My discussions with these scholars and scholar practitioners, and my observations of their dedication and support for their doctoral students, furthered and enhanced my own perspectives. Shannon Houston, the director of the department of educational leadership, helped me think through and operationalize many of the practices in our doctoral program that now serve as the foundation of this book. Her administrative skills, keen eye for detail, critical feedback, and support are deeply acknowledged and appreciated.

To my wife, Gitte, I am thankful that you saw so clearly how easy it was for me to talk and write about these topics, and how you thus encouraged and supported this work throughout. Finally, to Michaela and Matthias, it is with gratitude that, yes, yet again, Daddy was allowed to keep working on his book instead of playing another round of cards or participate in the backyard triple-overtime, penalty-kick tournament. Double-overtime was more than enough for these weary fingers.

# *About the Author*

**Dan W. Butin** is the founding dean of the school of education at Merrimack College. He is the editor and author of over fifty books, articles, and book chapters, including the books *Teaching Social Foundations of Education* and *Service-Learning and Social Justice Education.* Dr. Butin's research focuses on issues of educator preparation and policy and community engagement. Prior to working in higher education, Dr. Butin taught middle school and in an adult GED program and was the chief financial officer of Teach For America. More about Dr. Butin's teaching and scholarship can be found at http://danbutin.org.

# *Dedication*

This book would not have been possible without the struggles, joys,
and accomplishments of the doctoral students I have had the privilege of
working with at Cambridge College. I am humbled by their perseverance
toward a vision of a better world. They have shown me what they needed
from their doctoral studies, and it was the least that I could do to create it.
This book is thus but a small testament to them.

# 1

## *A Guide for Practitioner Scholars*

"I of course knew I was going to France for my semester abroad. I had studied French in my college courses. I took out books about France from the library. And then I got to France and I was shocked, literally shocked, that everyone was speaking French." One of our doctoral students—let's call her "Lynn"—was relating this story of surprise and frustration in one of our regular doctoral debriefing sessions as a way to make a very poignant point: she had really thought she knew what she was getting into when she enrolled in our doctoral program. She had read our program literature, spoken to colleagues who had gone through a doctoral program, and reflected upon her educational experiences to date and goals for the future. She knew that a doctoral degree was necessary for her career advancement (she was currently the curriculum design specialist in her district) and that she wanted to make a difference in how curricula were designed in her district and statewide. She was excited to begin the process and thought she was more than prepared.

But then, the realities started to pile up. At first, Lynn could not decide upon which dissertation topic to focus on. Then, even with strong support from her dissertation chair, she had a hard time narrowing her topic so it would be manageable and doable. She was now struggling to balance her full-time job, continue reading, and finalize her dissertation proposal. She would, she confided, sometimes fall asleep on the sofa while trying to read yet another journal article. There were knowing nods around the room as two-dozen educators—teachers, principals, school psychologists, and higher education administrators—heard their own situations being spoken out loud.

All of our doctoral students are seasoned and successful educators managing complex daily situations in classrooms, schools, and school districts across the country. They have advanced in the educational system, successfully completed graduate degrees, won awards and grants, and see themselves as change agents for educational renewal and social justice. They too thought they knew what they were getting into. All of our doctoral students came into the program thinking they were going to research and solve complex educational problems, gain deep knowledge in their specialization in order to become better teachers and leaders, overturn the inertia all too common in K–12 schools, and gain critical skills they could leverage to lead local educational reform and transform teaching and learning. Instead, they found themselves falling asleep on their sofas and questioning their ability to successfully complete their doctoral dissertations.

They are not alone. Nationally, more than half of all doctoral students drop out of their programs without ever completing their dissertation (Golde, 2005; Lovitts, 2001). (The more inclusive term "doctoral student" is used throughout this book since a "doctoral candidate" has technically completed all coursework and exams, passed the dissertation proposal, and is now "ABD," "all but dissertation.") Of those that finish, the average time-to-completion for a doctorate in education is over a decade (Planty et al., 2008). While the delivery and structure of K–12 education have fundamentally shifted over the last quarter century, much of doctoral education continues to operate through norms and practices that appear better suited for the nineteenth century when the doctoral degree first began being awarded in the United States. Our doctoral students are often, like most doctoral students in education, caught by what the philosopher and psychologist William James (1903) famously and derisively termed the "PhD octopus."

## QUESTIONING THE DOCTORATE

James (1903), writing at the cusp of the twentieth century when the doctoral degree was just gaining traction in higher education, was deeply critical of a trend where the skills, experience, and character of an individual were cast aside such that only "the three magical letters were the thing seriously required" (p. 1). In many ways, James was a proponent of doctoral education for spurring innovative research and helping, as he called it, "to gain bread-winning positions" for those undertaking the arduous process (p. 2). What James disdained was the formalization of a bureaucratic process that could, by the simple granting of a diploma, seemingly confer the aura of intellectual brilliance. This was, for James, not just charlatanism; it was the outright undermining of American principles of fairness in fostering "a tyrannical Machine with unforeseen powers of exclusion and corruption" (p. 2). Those who knew how to "play the game" and had the resources to do so could successfully receive a doctorate, whereas others potentially much more qualified but without insider knowhow or external support were deprived of this opportunity.

Unfortunately, James's fears have proven all too real a hundred years later. While the number of doctorates has dramatically increased—more than 40,000 are awarded each and every year—their value in actually helping to prepare the next generation of researchers, leaders, and teachers has never been more in question. Research across disciplines from the arts and humanities to the social and natural sciences has questioned the ability of the doctoral degree to adequately develop and nurture relevant skills (Golde & Dore, 2001; Golde & Walker, 2006; McWilliam, Lawson, & Evans, 2005). As one prominent report has noted (Woodrow Wilson Foundation, 2005), doctoral education, and its processes and practices, is fundamentally misaligned with many students' aspirations, careers, and real-world issues:

> The problem of a ridiculously long and costly number of years for earning the doctorate has many components, including an inertial tendency to require more and more, as if the doctorate is the last stage of knowing rather than a moment that leads beyond itself. (p. 6)

Doctoral programs in education are not immune from such criticism. In fact, a host of recent critiques (e.g., Hess & Kelly, 2005; Levin, 2006; Levine, 2005, 2007; Shulman et al., 2006) have argued that doctoral programs in education are fatally inadequate for teacher-leaders and administrators in bridging theory with practice and university knowledge with K–12 classroom realities. Moreover, the scholarship produced appears to be piecemeal and unable to answer pressing real-world questions. This, scholars suggest, is symptomatic of a long-standing stigma; the field of higher education views the educational doctorate as being the "poor cousin" of a "real" doctorate and without its own unique and legitimate identity, signature practices, and goals (Clifford & Guthrie, 1988; Labaree, 2004).

There have, of course, been attempts to rethink and rework the doctorate in education, dating back to almost the time it was first awarded—in 1893 as a PhD at Teachers College at Columbia University and in 1920 as an EdD at Harvard. Some scholars have suggested doing away with the PhD, while others have suggested the dismantling of the EdD (Deering, 1998; Orr, 2007; Osguthorpe & Wong, 1993). Some scholars have pointed to the dissertation format as the problem, while others find that the problem is the very nature of doctoral study (Barnett & Muth, 2008; Duke & Beck, 1999; Grogan, Donaldson, & Simmons, 2007; Pries, Grogan, Sherman, &

Beaty, 2007; Shulman, 2007). A host of recent scholarship, for example, has explicitly focused on shifting how institutions structure, support, and grant a doctorates in education (e.g., Archbald, 2008; Young, 2006) in order to develop doctoral programs better aligned with and supportive of practitioner scholars in education.

In part, all of these debates occur because the education dissertation lies at the crossroads of theory and practice. Traditionally, such a distinction was marked by the differentiation between an EdD (a "Doctor of Education") and a PhD (a "Doctor of Philosophy" in education). A PhD program in education is supposedly set up to prepare educational researchers who will immediately thereafter teach in higher education and focus on their research and teaching. EdD programs, on the other hand, are seen as preparing practicing educators who are then able to understand and apply theory to the immediate and important educational issues in front of them.

While higher education has traditionally privileged the so-called more scholarly path, there is, in fact, little evidence that a "life of the mind" is any more difficult than bringing theory to life. In fact, translating research into effective practice has consistently been the weak link within the educational research community. While it is usually true that spending five, six, or seven years immersed in a topic will produce expert knowledge, there is little research to suggest that a long dissertation (in terms of both time and pages) is a good dissertation. The debates and revisions to doctoral study in education can, as such, be understood as trying to solve the theory-practice divide of educational research and practice.

Such initiatives, however, no matter how worthwhile or genuine, cannot mask the continued problematic situation of the field. As one of the most scathing critics from inside the field (Levine, 2007) has argued, there is a lack of focus, rigor, and relevance for educators who may simply be using the doctoral degree as yet another stepping stone in their administrative enhancement. Levine's study found an appalling sense of rigor or quality in the preparation of educational researchers: "Deans and faculty, even at the highest-ranked schools of education, persistently complained that their doctoral curriculums did not equip students sufficiently for the dissertation" (p. 34); students seemed to have minimal understanding of research methods or paradigms; almost half of all doctoral recipients thought their doctoral curriculum lacked rigor; and "many of the faculty members advising doctoral students today are not productive scholars and lack the skills, knowledge and experience necessary to mentor students in preparing a substantial piece of research" (p. 55). Even more damning, Levine's study found that many education dissertations were weak, asked trivial research questions, used improper and shoddy methodology, collected and analyzed data improperly, drew conclusions inconsistent with the data, were poorly written, and were "so short as to appear stunted and superficial, the sort of thing that might suffice for a class project" (p. 58).

This is harsh criticism; it, unfortunately, is not unique either to education or to the current state of the field (e.g., Cleary, 2000; Geiger, 1997; White, 1986). Part of the criticism, it should be noted, is not necessarily focused on the education doctorate per se. It just so happens that the last two decades have seen a profound addition to the doctoral landscape. Doctoral degrees in education offered through nontraditional doctoral programs in traditional institutions, as well as through for-profit institutions, have become significantly more prevalent. While these programs graduate only a small percentage of the 6,000 to 7,000 doctoral degrees conferred yearly in education, their growth has been dramatic and noticeable.

Specifically, a hybrid or even fully online structure is deeply appealing to practitioners and may be noticeably better at supporting genuine learning (Ghezzi, 2007; Ivankova & Stick, 2007; Sherman & Beaty, 2007). Yet, it is also understandable how such nontraditional formats (i.e., doctoral coursework done primarily online; minimal face-to-face interaction between a dissertation chair, doctoral committee, and doctoral student) raise questions about the quality and value of a doctoral degree. Given such tumultuous changes and critiques from within and outside of the educational field, there is no longer a clear vision of what qualifies as a legitimate and valuable dissertation, what form doctoral programs and dissertations should take, and how these dissertations can positively contribute to the later success of students. And, unfortunately again, doctoral students are caught in the middle of all of this.

## SEEING THE DOCTORAL PROCESS THROUGH DOCTORAL STUDENTS' EYES

In one respect, Lynn and our other doctoral students can intuitively relate to this feeling of being caught in a situation not of their own making. They are attempting to write a highly formulaic manuscript, in a very prescribed style, for an audience of just four people. They must demonstrate particular "skills" through this manuscript that will most likely never be asked for again. They would, moreover, need to spend an inordinate amount of time and energy in rethinking and revising this manuscript if they ever wanted to use it for any other audience. It is, thus, not hard to understand why both the national dropout rate and cynicism may be so high in doctoral programs in education.

And yet, this is not the whole story. After Lynn had finished comparing her experience in France to her doctoral process, another doctoral student spoke up. She too now fell asleep on her sofa, and, she informed us with a laugh, this was highly ironic since she had been yelling at her husband for years not to do that. Interestingly, however, the reason she fell asleep—reading books and articles on her dissertation topic after long days as a special education coordinator—was actually empowering. She was doing exactly what we told her a doctoral student should be doing at that stage in the process; she was reading every day, jotting down notes, writing summaries and critiques of what she read, and compiling a longer and longer bibliography. She knew it was slow going, but she could see her notes getting longer, her ideas getting sharper, and her brain making easier connections across topics and ideas. At work, she caught herself using phrases such as "as the research suggests" and "how can we operationalize that idea?" Falling asleep on the sofa, in fact, had become an informal sign of victory for her. She was continuing to move forward, to push herself, and in the process, she would naturally fall asleep from exhaustion. All the while, the next stage in the process was visible in the distance. This perspective brought widespread nodding from her cohort, and afterwards, Lynn agreed that, yes, she too was making progress. It was hard, but doable.

An anecdote, I tell my students, does not count as data. I do not mean to exaggerate this onetime event as some Shangri-La of doctoral achievement—except this was not a onetime event. In fact, the doctoral program that these students are part of boasts an 80 percent completion rate. Students pass their dissertation proposals within five months of starting the process, and successfully defend their dissertations an average of twelve months later. Graduates have gone on to teach at top-tier colleges and universities, advanced to high administrative positions in their districts, and become teacher-leaders in their schools and school districts. Our population of doctoral students, moreover, is overwhelmingly first-generation college graduates and 65 percent nonwhite. Our students are extremely motivated, as a doctoral degree is a milestone achievement for themselves and their careers. But, it is more than just their individual drive and perseverance that can explain such success.

A host of research supports the fact that doctoral completion has much more to do with the structural conditions at an institution than anything personal about the individual (Gardner, 2008; Goenner & Snaith, 2004; Golde, 2005; Lovitts, 2005; Malone, Nelson, & Nelson, 2004). In some ways, the unique structure of our doctoral program does in fact enhance the quality and timeliness of our students' success. With a concurrent dissertation-design model, students take specific research courses while they simultaneously design their research and collect and analyze data. They continue in a cohort group throughout the entire process, including the dissertation writing stage to enhance academic and emotional support, and receive ample one-on-one meetings and support from the dissertation chair.

More relevant, though, is the program's ultimate structure around, and focus on, creating a way for professional and experienced educators to display their skills and strengths while still undergoing a rigorous academic program to help them successfully conduct and write a doctoral-quality dissertation.

I teach the first course in the doctoral curriculum, Introduction to the Dissertation, as well as lead the dissertation seminar course taken each semester by all of the students as long as they stay in the cohort. This seminar (where Lynn spoke up) is a combination of debriefing, peer support, discussion of strategies for success, and readings about the dissertation process. In each of these courses and sessions, I very consciously provide detailed and concrete strategies to support our students' ultimate success (e.g., clarifying theoretical frameworks and research designs, discussing the minutiae of APA style and bibliographic reference tools, strategizing library research skills and the most effective means by which to do a literature review). But irrespective of which topic I am lecturing about or leading a discussion on, I focus on making visible the implicit norms of academic work, what is oftentimes termed the "implicit" or "hidden" curriculum.

This is a crucial component because doctoral students are rarely told about this. A so-called "traditional" dissertation is done by a full-time doctoral student who spends all of his time reading and researching in the library, writing at his computer, taking doctoral courses with other full-time students, and meeting occasionally with his advisor. In such a scenario, this doctoral student comes to understand the nature of academic work almost by osmosis. He lives it and sees it all around him. The knowledge he doesn't pick up in the first year or two can always be gained in the next few years or from other doctoral students a few years ahead who offer guidance and advice. Even then, he may graduate with large gaps of knowledge.

This is what is traditionally known as the doctoral "journey," and there are numerous how-to books, Web sites, and advice columns on how to survive such an "expedition" and make the most of it. The journey is portrayed as an exciting, albeit grueling, adventure, where stumbles, scraped knees, and diversions are just "par for the course," a seemingly enjoyable and necessary part of the trip. Most advice from such a "journey" perspective attempts to point out guideposts along the way and provide with suggestions of where not to drink the water.

The problem with this vision and accompanying advice is that the vast majority of doctoral students in education don't follow this type of path nor gain from such a "school of hard knocks" attitude mixed with anecdotal "war stories" of past practices. This is because the dissertation is not a journey; it is a process. This is not a semantic quibbling over terms. A journey is a trip with minimal guidance, direction, or goals. Before people start a journey, they are wished luck and asked to keep in touch. They may even be offered advice with stories about a well-wisher's own journey, presuming that such experiences may transfer to the forthcoming situation. But, this is not how one thinks about a process. A process has definable starting and ending points, as well as numerous points in between. A process has particular and idiosyncratic characteristics that can be better understood and worked out through specific, heuristic models. One may not be able to predict or prepare for every occurrence, but good models and strategies can account for and help us to understand the vast majority of options and alternatives in a well-defined process. And, the dissertation is indeed a well-defined process.

Long ago, Dewey (1916) noted that a good teacher cannot truly teach a lesson or unit if she has not first thought through the ends of the process before starting at the very beginning. Understanding the end goals of the process can help us work backward to develop the most effective and efficient means by which to begin. The students may not realize why the teacher introduces what she does at the point she does, but a good teacher knows the relevant issues and key junctures at each stage of the lesson. It is likely this perspective that Lynn and most other doctoral students in education want: a means to support their objectives through academically rigorous yet time-efficient means.

We must remember, most doctoral students in education are not typical doctoral students. National data (Planty et al., 2008) show that doctoral recipients in education are on average age 42 (the oldest by far of any other field) and have over a decade of work experience. More than 60 percent of doctoral recipients in education are married; they are also the least likely group of all doctoral fields to have had parents with postsecondary education, with 59 percent of fathers and 67 percent of mothers without college degrees.

Put otherwise, most doctoral students in education are already experienced and excellent educators who do not have the desire or resources to spend ten years wandering around the hallways and byways of academia. Rather, doctoral students in education want to be treated as the adults whom they are. Adult learning theory (e.g., Keeton, Sheckley, & Griggs, 2002; Mezirow, 1981, 1997; Tisdell, 1998) presumes that adult students are engaged learners who bring detailed and useful practitioner knowledge and positionality to their studies; in other words, doctoral students are experienced educational practitioners needing a specific content and context to demonstrate acquired skill sets and the ability to transfer such skill sets to academic research contexts (Labaree, 2003). The fact, moreover, that these doctoral students tend to be about ten years older than doctoral students in other fields is not a simple temporal distinction, since those years "in the field" provide educators with maturity, a wealth of valuable insights and professional expertise in teaching and learning, and the opportunity for moving into and successfully rising in the administrative ranks.

Yet, there is minimal acknowledgement that doctoral study can be daunting for those who have been out of school for more than ten years and may not have the requisite graduate skills even if they have other skills and passion. Adult learning theory (e.g., Mezirow, 1997) is clear here that programs must move beyond a deficit model in order to offer "a rationale for selecting appropriate educational practices and actively resisting social and cultural forces that distort and delimit adult learning" (Mezirow, 1997, p. 12). If the challenge of doctoral study in education is transforming successful educational practitioners into educational researchers and scholar practitioners, then a solution through the frame of adult learning theory must arise organically by from designing processes and protocols "that deliberately demonstrate respect for the skills and orientations that teachers bring with them" (Labaree, 2003, p. 21).

This "respect," it should be noted, is not simply the respect for the skills and aptitudes of the master teacher or visionary administrator. Another aspect to the national data is that many doctoral students in education—by the very nature of the fact that they are first-generation college graduates or the first in their families to pursue graduate studies—do not have the requisite "cultural capital" necessary for success. This is what William James (1903) referred to as some doctoral students being excluded and deprived of opportunities.

Cultural capital refers to the practices, norms, and patterns of particular groups of individuals. It is oftentimes used in educational research to discuss the differential academic success between students coming from low and high-income families. Pierre Bourdieu (Bourdieu & Passeron, 1990), a French sociologist who first popularized this concept, found, for example, that there was a direct correlation between the types of readings a family would do and the success of their children in school. This was not about some children having greater access to books or hearing more words every day and thus doing better in school. This was about the fact that children of parents who read "high culture" materials—what we would equate with *The New York Times* or *Harper's Magazine*—did better than those who read "low culture" materials. Bourdieu's argument, documented by dozens of studies thereafter, is that schools only reward certain types of culture (Delpit, 1995; Ogbu, 1970). To put it somewhat simplistically, the way one talks and dresses and the references one makes (whether it's to NPR or NASCAR), dramatically impacts whether one will be academically successful.

This is equally true in higher education as it is in K–12 schools. There are a multitude unspoken rules and norms in higher education, and oftentimes we don't even know where to begin to ask questions or what types of questions to ask. The problem is that while doctoral programs and advisors may spend a lot of time on the explicit aspects of doctoral study, there is usually very little guidance concerning the implicit and oftentimes the most important part: how do I actually make it through this process? This is what this book is about.

## THIS BOOK AS GUIDELINES AND GUARDRAILS

Just as I do with my doctoral students in my courses and as a dissertation chair, this book provides a detailed and concrete protocol for successfully completing your dissertation. It provides strategies and perspectives about what to do at key stages in the dissertation process, and how to do it. Lynn and her cohort, and many other doctoral students, have substantial skills and experiences. They are motivated and focused. What they all too often don't have, though, are the guidelines and "guardrails" to use as a starting point. Specifically, doctoral students—as mature, experienced, and self-motivated adults—are looking for a starting point with specific yet flexible parameters from which they can get their own bearings to move forward.

This is not a cookie-cutter approach to writing a dissertation. There is no such thing. A dissertation is an in-depth and rigorous examination of a particular issue that provides new knowledge and/or perspectives and, as such, contributes to ongoing scholarship and discussion around that issue. I cannot write that for you. What I can do, though, is offer support and scaffolding, providing you with freedom to focus your valuable time and energy on what matters: the content of your dissertation idea. To take an analogous example, nobody complains that all doctoral programs are cookie-cutter approaches because they all have a more-or-less standardized format: coursework, comprehensive exams, and the writing of a dissertation. Everyone understands that the standardization lies in the structure, allowing individuals to focus on the particular specifics of the content they want to focus on, in what order, and from what perspective.

Another way to think about this book is as the equivalent to a mnemonic or what is referred to as the ability to "chunk" information. Researchers who study the transformation of learners from novice to expert practitioners have shown that what separates chess masters from novice players is not the master player's ability to more quickly work through all the possible moves on the board and predict their long-term consequences (technically referred to as the greater breadth and depth of search); rather, chess masters were much more adept at "chunking" chess configurations and thus knowing quickly which were fruitful for further consideration. While novices spent equal time working through as many possible moves as time allowed, chess masters immediately focused on the limited set of moves they deemed relevant for the situation at hand (Chase & Simon, 1973; de Groot, 1965).

The point here is that there are concrete and highly effective strategies for maximizing learning, and how we learn about one thing is transferable to how we learn about other things (Bransford, Brown, & Cocking, 2000). *The strategies in this book are not the dissertation.* The mnemonic of "please excuse my dear Aunt Sally" to learn the order of mathematical operations (parenthesis, exponents, multiplication, division, addition, subtraction) is a wonderful teaching tool; it does not, though, automatically turn students into mathematicians. It is a tool. Likewise, this book provides mechanisms that allow you to maximize your learning curve for how to think and write about your research passion.

This specificity and structure is particularly critical for educators who continue to juggle their studies with their professional career and are not full-time graduate students. For, unfortunately, too many doctoral programs provide too much latitude for their doctoral students. It is of course valuable to take a wide range of elective courses or to read widely and deeply on fascinating and important educational topics. Nevertheless, the point is that the advocacy of "flexibility" and "following your (academic) whims" is too often shorthand for not having a program structure or advising capacity that carefully guides doctoral students in a timely and effective manner through the necessary stages of the dissertation process.

This book, moreover, provides a strong scaffolding exactly because there is all too often minimal guidance and minimal understanding of the exact type of focus that doctoral students need. Part of this may be due to professors frequently being busy with their own research, teaching, and advancement in their disciplinary field or at their own institutions. Many doctoral faculty advise anywhere between ten to thirty doctoral dissertations at any one time (Golde, 2000). Additionally, and no matter how well meaning an advisor may be, many faculty have minimal experience in the time-intensive process of helping focus dissertation ideas.

Research consistently shows that while mentoring is the single most critical component for on-time and quality dissertation completion, few faculty know how to be an effective mentor and advisor (Kam, 1997; Richardson, 2006; Rosen & Bates, 1967; Spillett & Moisiewicz, 2004). A recent study of social science PhD graduates (Council on Graduate Schools PhD Completion Project, 2008, p. 28), for example, found that just over half of all respondents were "very satisfied" with how their dissertation chair helped develop their thesis topic and their guidance in completing the dissertation. While very few (under 6 percent) were "very unsatisfied," it is troubling that more than 40 percent of doctoral students were just "somewhat satisfied" or "somewhat unsatisfied." You wouldn't think that this could be possible; professors are supposed to be intelligent individuals. They are. But, guiding doctoral students toward a clear, concise, and meaningful dissertation topic and then transforming that idea into a doable research project is a very different art form than mastering specific statistical techniques or being an expert in a specific educational subfield.

It should, of course, be acknowledged that simply reading this book will not miraculously allow you to pass the dissertation defense. This book is not snake oil, and no such promises can be made. To that end, I should also note that while this book is structured to maximize your focus and learning, I have to make some assumptions about you, the reader, and the dissertation process you are about to begin or already are on.

The first assumption is that you are indeed writing a traditional dissertation. While this may seem obvious, there is in fact a growing movement in higher education for nontraditional dissertations, ranging from action-research projects to multiple "articles" to a portfolio-capstone project (e.g., Grogan et al., 2007; Shulman et al., 2006). These are important developments in the field, yet they operate from different assumptions and with different goals; as such, these types of alternative dissertation formats are not discussed.

My second assumption is that while this may be one of the first books you read as you prepare for and engage in your dissertation process, it is certainly not the only one. This book cannot substitute for the knowledge gained from your research courses or advising sessions. While I cover many of the basics about, for example, research design, the Institutional Review Board (IRB), and structuring a literature review, this book is meant as a companion rather than a replacement for your own coursework and in-depth readings. If your advisor suggests a specific book, read it. If your graduate department requires a specific protocol, follow it. This book is meant to help you "chunk" your resources of time and energy so that you actually know the questions to ask your advisor, the most fruitful way to structure your literature review, and the most productive way through the process in your particular institution. It is a guide along that path, not a substitute for it.

A final assumption is that, obviously, I do not know what your dissertation is about. I do not know if it is exploring gender issues in elementary-mathematics classrooms or the role of emotional intelligence in leadership preparation. I do not know if you are taking a qualitative or quantitative approach to your research design. And, I do not know the type or amount of data you plan on collecting, or how you will go about analyzing and writing about these data. I am, as they say, flying blind.

But that doesn't mean I can't offer highly helpful strategies for success. "Flying blind" is actually common practice in the aviation world. It is known as "instrument flying," rather than "visual flying" and occurs whenever the pilot cannot see visual cues due to poor weather, clouds, or other problems. Pilots thus rely on their instrument panel and their years of honed experience to get them through the vast majority of situations that they may encounter. Similarly, this book draws on a large array of academic research to provide the key indicators for what constitutes a quality dissertation and how to get there. It synthesizes my own and many other academics' experiences in guiding dissertations and the best means to do so. Thus, while I cannot know your specific situation, the academic literature provides very good estimations of the major challenges and hurdles for doctoral students and, likewise, the best means to support them.

## STRATEGIES FOR SUCCESS

My goal, then, is to increase your awareness of the key issues to address in your dissertation and then to give you the tools and strategies for success. This is critical because the dissertation is (or should be) a "different beast" from any other educational endeavor you have ever undertaken. The problem, actually, is not so much that a dissertation is in fact a different beast; the problem is that no one usually talks to doctoral students about how and why it is so different, or what can be done to deal with such differences. For this reason, let me provide two quick examples to illustrate this focus on tangible support for success (these examples are discussed in-depth in later chapters).

The first is the question of what constitutes a quality dissertation. Since there is no single or easy answer, professors oftentimes sidestep this question (if doctoral students even know how to ask it in such a direct and forthright way) with the refrain "I know it when I see it." While this sounds pithy, it is of no help for the doctoral student attempting to find his way through what appears to be an infinite number of options, and the options themselves seem to have an infinite number of permutations. It leaves the doctoral student either to place everything in the trust of the dissertation chair or search for some "lowest common factor" such as the number of pages, which itself is ultimately of no use. I could, for example, tell you that research indicates a typical education dissertation is approximately 150 pages long, with a standard deviation of about 20 pages—meaning that 95 percent of all dissertations are between 110 and 190 pages. However, this information is of little help if you write 180 pages of jumbled prose.

So instead, at the beginning of my introductory course, I provide my students with some basic guidelines of both the big picture and specific examples of what counts as a quality dissertation. The attributes I provide (e.g., a quality dissertation has to have a nontrivial topic that can withstand the "so what?" question) offer students specific terminology and a conceptual overview closed-ended enough to be meaningful yet open-ended enough to foster their own growth and flourish within these parameters. More importantly, students can now use these parameters both as boundaries to be respected as well as limits to be pushed: "Is this really a nontrivial topic?" they can ask a committee member; "How exactly do my survey questions help me to answer my research question?" they can ask their dissertation chair. The articulation of specific guidelines provides a clear starting point and flexible "guardrails" within which students can now move forward.

The other quick example pertains to the table of contents. The table of contents is the skeleton, the fundamental structure, of your dissertation. Although it is just one or two pages, a good table of contents should quickly provide the reader with a sense of the logical structure, progression, and details of the dissertation. Yet, most doctoral students wait until the very end of the dissertation process to create their table of contents, since, they believe, they first need to figure out all of the different sections in their dissertation before they can put it into a table of contents.

This is in fact completely backward. The table of contents should be the very first thing you create. The reality is that most tables of contents have very similar structures. While some differences exist between qualitative

## Hint! What Exactly Does a Quality Dissertation Look Like?

Educational researchers (e.g., Di Pierro, 2007; Holbrook Bourke, Lovat, & Fairbarn, 2008; Lovitts, 2005; Winter, Griffiths, & Green, 2000) suggest that all quality dissertations, irrespective of their research focus, methodology, or theoretical framework, have a set of common attributes:

**They are nontrivial.** A quality dissertation is nontrivial in the sense that it examines a potentially valuable research topic that can inform understanding, practice, or policy of a particular issue. While there is no easy way to answer whether any particular topic is nontrivial (this is, after all, why you need the expertise of your dissertation chair), the dissertation must be able to answer the "so what?" question of relevance and contextualize the issue within a broader field of research and discussion.

**They are theoretically and methodologically explicit and clear.** A quality dissertation can clearly articulate the basis for and procedure of analysis. A theoretical framework clarifies why the dissertation looks at one thing rather than another; the research design clarifies how the data were collected and analyzed. The key for each is not to cover everything and anything; in fact, it is usually quite the opposite: the goal is to be clear and explicit about the limitations of the dissertation so the reader understands the boundaries of inquiry.

**Research methods are appropriate to the research questions.** Different research questions necessitate different methodological techniques for data collection and analysis. This is true across different forms of qualitative and quantitative research. The techniques—be it statistical analyses, interviews, surveys, or fieldwork—should be adequate to gather the data actually needed to answer the questions.

**Conclusions are based on the data.** It is tempting but inappropriate to overreach in articulating one's conclusions in order to substantiate a particular worldview, policy, or practice. A quality dissertation, though, can only make conclusions based on an analysis of the gathered data.

**They are analytic.** A quality dissertation is more than a simple descriptive, formulaic, and/or rhetorical document. It cannot be a compilation of anecdotes, research practices, or synopses. It must examine and question the research literature, analyze and synthesize data, and provide a coherent and thoughtful evaluation of the research within the larger context of the study.

and quantitative dissertations (since qualitative dissertations have more flexibility concerning the number and structuring of chapters), most dissertations should have five specific chapters, and these should be broken down into specific sections and subsections. For example, quantitative dissertations usually need a subsection on the validity and reliability of the instrumentation used; qualitative dissertations usually need a subsection on the ethics of fieldwork. By creating such sections and subsections at the very beginning of the dissertation process, a doctoral student will be much more focused and clear about what must be researched and thought through in the specific dissertation.

I am, of course, aware that even the best strategies may not prevent some doctoral students from calling it quits. Research suggests that two-thirds of all doctoral students drop out either right before or right after the start of the dissertation stage in their doctoral programs (Lovitts, 2001). There are naturally many reasons this may happen that have nothing to do with academic difficulties. Sometimes, "life happens." There are life situations that none of us can prepare for and that derail any and all plans we may have for our careers, education, and future. One of our doctoral students, for example, was called up by his army reserve unit to go to Iraq just before the start of his program. Another doctoral student lost her mother and then her father within the span of two months. These are traumatic situations that overwhelm even the most dedicated student.

Sometimes, students just procrastinate. This occurs with a complicated mix of personality traits, life conditions, and educational contexts. Sometimes, such procrastination—in the right context—is actually a highly positive response. In the middle of my own writing, I may decide that the dishes have to be done right now; or, perhaps I take a day or two to do other academic tasks that do not appear as never-ending. I have learned that these situations are my way of processing the enormous mix of data, ideas, and tangents I am struggling to comprehend and put into a logical argument. So I do the dishes, and my brain (whether I know it or not) spins and spins and spins. When I sit down again, I am (hopefully) able to write about what seemed impossible before. Yet, sometimes such procrastination becomes severe and ongoing, with weeks and months passing without the student able to sit down and write. The longer this occurs, the more likely that the student will drop out.

While all of the above may contribute to difficulties or the inability to move forward, the most documented reason for students' lack of success is a fundamental misalignment between what they think they are going to do and what they actually have to do to finish the dissertation. Part of this misalignment is that none of us were ever truly prepared for doctoral study by our educational system. Every other educational level presumes that the student is primarily and fundamentally a user of research. For the first time, you will produce your own research with your own voice. This is scary. You must now come up with your own research study. Most students have no problem doing the coursework. Many make it through the comprehensive exams with flying colors. But, that's the easy part—easy because in such tasks (taking coursework or passing exams) someone else has created the agenda and set up the process. A dissertation is about taking *your* ideas and passions and translating them into a realistic and doable project.

Moreover, this process is a scary one because to receive a doctoral degree is to become a part of a community of scholars. While all doctoral programs differ across disciplines and institutions, what is constant is the emphasis on careful and rigorous analysis of a particular issue and the attempt to produce new knowledge. The analysis—through a comprehensive literature review, distinct theoretical framework, and a focused research question and subsequent methodologically sophisticated examination—offers an opportunity for the doctoral student to immerse himself in a "culture of thoughtfulness" that does not simply accept received truths, assumed doctrines, or immediate reactions. As the Nobel Prize–winning scientist Richard Feynman once wryly noted, the definition of science (and, perhaps, doctoral studies in general) is "the belief in the ignorance of authority" (as cited in Berliner, 2002, p. 18). Truth, from such a perspective, has to be achieved one careful and deliberate step at a time.

This "truth," moreover, is never complete. The literary theorist Stanley Fish (2008) has long argued that what sets higher education apart from all other institutions is its constant and never-ending search for truth, wherever this path may lead. More importantly, Fish argues that "truth," irrespective of discipline or topic, must be understood as a verb rather than a noun. One doesn't just find a "truth," accept it, and move on. What is "true" is a process of debate, analysis and reanalysis, formulation and reformulation, ad infinitum. Something is "true" so long as it can be questioned, built upon, or discarded. Put otherwise, once something is no longer questioned, it is not truth. It is dogma. As such, the creation of "new knowledge" at the heart of a doctoral dissertation is nothing more (or less) than the entrance into and participation within a long-standing discussion about a specific issue. The discussion may have been going on for thirty or three hundred or even three thousand years (as is often the case in philosophy). What is important for you to understand is that you have now stepped into this discussion. Your contribution is your dissertation.

What this really means is that all of my doctoral students who come in believing that the dissertation will finally, finally, give them the answers to solve all of their problems are sadly disappointed. They will certainly gain immensely in learning about cutting-edge research, thinking carefully and thoroughly about a particular topic, and realizing the multifaceted components of complex educational issues. But, they will not find the "truth." They will not save the world.

What they ultimately do with their dissertation and their newfound skills may indeed help a lot of people in a lot of ways. This is, in fact, what I believe it means to be a practitioner scholar. It means being cognizant of the complexity around you while nevertheless moving forward in your daily practices. It is about being what Schön (1983) calls a reflective practitioner, someone able to reflect both about practice and in practice. It is about taking the best research available, knowing how to think about it, and using it in your particular context and situation, and within context-specific limitations. This is a learned way of thinking, and the dissertation can be thought of as the proxy, the process, to help you become that kind of thinker and actor. A dissertation is about helping you to become a practitioner scholar. In order to do so, the dissertation must be understood as a process to accomplish.

A doctoral degree is the culminating milestone in American higher education, and the doctoral dissertation is the visible manifestation of its achievement. Yet, the goal of this book is not simply to help you just finish. A bound dissertation sitting on your bookshelf should indeed be a goal, but it is the skills gained through the process of making that vision a reality that is truly the heart of the dissertation.

The dissertation process should help you focus how you think about complex and contested issues, strengthen your ability to carefully and systematically investigate the relevant research, clarify how to disentangle variables and frame the key issues, and marshal relevant data to substantiate your conclusions. This should all occur not only about the specific issue you will investigate for your dissertation, but also for every other issue you tackle as a practitioner scholar ever after. This book provides the intellectual frameworks, the guided activities, the research-based models, the heuristic processes, and the concrete examples to accomplish all of that. So it's just fine, like Lynn, to lie down on the sofa and keep reading. Let's begin.

# 2

## *A Roadmap From Start to Finish*

While it may be more than a little strange to acknowledge, you are more or less starting over when you get to the dissertation stage of your doctoral program. Sure, you have taken lots of courses. Many may even have been about your dissertation idea, and more than a few were supposed to have prepared you for the methodological aspects of qualitative or quantitative research. You also have probably been through some comprehensive exams where you wrote on a range of educational topics to demonstrate the breadth and depth of your knowledge. Yet, as you begin to mull over your actual dissertation, it might be strategically helpful to accept that you are truly at the beginning of the process, again.

This may seem absurd given the immense amount of time (and money) a doctoral student has already invested in her education. So, getting through the dissertation is an entirely different game than making it through the doctoral process to this point in time. Malcolm Gladwell (2008), for example, has shown how it is almost impossible to gauge the success of professional quarterbacks from their past success in college football. What the quarterback has so far encountered in the college game, Gladwell argues, has very little resemblance to what he will play at the professional level; as such, the level of success for a future professional quarterback, no matter how seemingly high in college, has little, if any, bearing on his ultimate future in the NFL. Gladwell points out that this is because the new environment in the NFL is at a fundamentally different level with different norms of play; put simply, professional athletes play at a level far above even top-ranked college football.

In a similar vein, while we have all written undergraduate and graduate research papers, it is necessary to understand the different level of play with the doctoral dissertation. This chapter thus offers guidance in preparing for this process and highlights key strategies for structuring your time, thinking, and work. Specifically, by "starting over," you have the chance to structure a process to fit your particular skills, timeframe, and constraints, rather than the other way around. The last thing you want to happen is for the dissertation process to slowly but surely overwhelm you. This chapter, then, walks you through each step of the process from start to finish—developing a tentative timeline for your dissertation, providing a framework for setting benchmarks along the way, and creating a table of contents.

To be blunt, the real goal of this chapter is to help you organize the next twelve to eighteen months of your life. This is not as obsessive-compulsive as it may sound. Structuring your time, thinking, and energy now is a strategic decision that will ultimately help you keep your sanity as you juggle home, work, and your dissertation research. Without such a structure, you would not be at the beginning of the dissertation process; you would be at the beginning of dropping out. For, as one of my doctoral students quipped upon realizing the extent of the research ahead, "By the end of this process, I'll either be a doctor or a patient!" A doctoral dissertation is simply too big to "wing it." You have to carefully, methodically, and systematically prepare for the process.

## THE BIG PICTURE

### An Outline of the Process

A dissertation comprises many steps, some discrete and many overlapping. Oftentimes, a dissertation is thought and talked about as a linear and straightforward process: a research question leads to a literature review, which leads to a methodological framework, which leads to collecting and analyzing data, which concludes with writing up the results and then defending the dissertation. This makes the process appear logical, doable, and easy to follow. And, from thirty thousand feet high, this is indeed how the process looks. But on the ground, the reality is much more iterative, recursive, and complex. Before delving into the complexities and subtleties of this process, let's lay out a traditional dissertation path.

Completing a dissertation can be thought of as moving through three distinct and successive steps: a preparation stage, a research stage, and a completion stage (see Figure 2.1). While the activities within each stage may not be so clear-cut and linear, the stages themselves are in fact unidirectional. In other words, you can't go backward once you've crossed from one stage to the next. This seemingly simple dictum has some pretty powerful implications for the dissertation process. First, it means that the initial stage in the process, the preparation stage, is of critical importance.

| Figure 2.1 | Overview of the Dissertation Process: A Three-Stage Model |

| **Preparation Stage** |
| --- |
| 1.  Set up your research. |
| 2.  Focus your research. |
| 3.  Prepare for the dissertation proposal. |
| 4.  Submit dissertation proposal. |
| 5.  Submit IRB (upon proposal approval). |
| **Research Stage** |
| 6.  Collect data. |
| 7.  Continue research and seek support. |
| 8.  Conduct data analysis. |
| 9.  Write first draft of dissertation. |
| **Completion Stage** |
| 10.  Write complete draft and submit to advisor for initial approval. |
| 11.  Prepare for dissertation defense. |
| 12.  Defend dissertation. |
| 13.  Finish |

Abraham Lincoln is quoted, in one version or another, of saying, "Give me six hours to chop down a tree and I will spend the first four sharpening the axe." The preparation stage is when you structure your thinking, focus your research questions, and argue coherently and cohesively that your dissertation research is both relevant and doable. The preparation stage will guide all of your subsequent research, data collection, and thinking. If it is not done right, all subsequent work will be tainted.

I oftentimes use the metaphor of a shooting range to help my doctoral students understand exactly how critical this stage is in the dissertation process. If I am shooting at a target five feet away, it doesn't make much difference if I shake slightly up or down, left or right; I'm going to hit near the center of the target simply by the virtue of being so close. But if I'm one hundred or one thousand feet away from the target, every minuscule movement will have an immense and ever-expanding impact. What was just an inch difference at five feet becomes a foot difference at a hundred feet. Expert marksmen, in fact, are taught to shoot in between breaths so that even the minute movement of breathing does not affect the shot.

This is exactly the same at the preparation stage. Making a slight error in how I frame my research questions, phrase my interview questions, or decide who should take the survey will have a magnified impact on the kind of data I collect and how I subsequently analyze it. And exactly because I can't go back, there is truly no other way to redo my mistake other than starting all over again. Few of us want to even think about that possibility.

This is why—to jump ahead just slightly in the process—the dissertation committee views the dissertation proposal as the most important stage in the entire process. It is the moment of final quality control when the committee has its last chance to shape your future path. It is an implicit contract between student and committee about what will be done, and how, throughout data collection and analysis. Once you pass the dissertation proposal, you have left the safety of the harbor and are out on your own. Of course, you can still get advice and feedback make modifications to your research design and continue to read and rethink and revise. But, your research questions and research direction are more or less set, and you have to follow them through to the end. This is just as true for a qualitative "emergent" research design—one that develops within the particular research context—as it is with the most standardized quantitative protocol. Chapter 6 discusses how to think about and deal with problematic or negative findings in your dissertation research, but it is much better to deal with the problems at the preparation stage, while they are still minor and tentative, rather than when they have blown up into make-or-break dilemmas at the dissertation defense.

A second implication of the unidirectional aspect of the process is that you can only collect the data you are prepared to collect. Later chapters will include the details of research design, data collection, and analysis. For now, the critical point is that you will usually have only one chance to collect the key data for your dissertation. This "one chance" may of course be a set of three or four interviews spaced out over many months. Yet, it is still "one chance" in the sense that everything should be focused around your specific research questions. If your questions are too vague or the answers too abstract, you're stuck. Once a survey is sent out, there is no way to get it back to add that one last question you realized you really needed.

Finally, your conclusions will only be powerful if your introduction is as well. This means that the impact and relevance of your dissertation actually hinges on how it is initially framed, rather than on the actual data you ultimately collect and the conclusions you finally draw. If you frame your dissertation as part of a larger discussion relevant and critical to a specific issue, then your conclusions will also have resonance.

The overall dissertation process should, therefore, be thought about as three distinct and self-contained stages. The preparation stage is when you develop your topic, focus your research questions, and write up a dissertation proposal explaining the theoretical framework, reviewing relevant literature, and detailing the methodological process that you will undertake in your data collection and analysis. Just like Lincoln's axe, I spend a disproportionate amount of time scaffolding this stage of the process for my doctoral students, and Chapters 3 and 4 are devoted to this critical stage. If you are successful here, the rest of the process will be much easier.

The second stage of research, usually thought of as the "real" part of the dissertation process, is where one collects, analyzes, and writes up the data. Oftentimes, if the dissertation proposal is extremely focused and specific, this is the easiest part of the dissertation process. One simply collects the data—by surveys, interviews, or observations—analyzes it, and writes up the basic results. This, of course, is easier said than done. There are myriad challenges in daily life that cause complications in all aspects of this process. A researcher may have to redo a set of interviews, revise observation protocols due to changes in school practices, or add a completely new section to the research design in order to take into account an unexpected development or finding. The basics of these situations are covered in Chapter 5.

The collection of all of the data and subsequent write-up leads to the third and final stage of the dissertation process. While different institutions have different protocols, everything revolves around the dissertation defense. The last two chapters of this book delve into the key details of putting everything together into a coherent and powerful narrative, as well as discuss what happens at the defense and afterward. For now, it is enough to state that if you have done everything correctly, your defense will actually be an enjoyable opportunity to have an in-depth and informed discussion with other academics (i.e., your committee) who have actually taken the time to carefully read and think about a topic that has been at the heart of your life for a year or more. This is truly a unique occasion and one that you should fully embrace, even if you think you are going to be too nervous to do so. It is not often that something you have been intellectually obsessed with for so long (and a dissertation can certainly be classified as an obsession) can be given the time for deliberate and deliberative discussion and reflection.

This process can, in turn, be mapped onto the standard five-chapter structure of a dissertation (see Figure 2.2). For now, this visualization gives you an overview of where you are going. The structure may at first appear arbitrary; at some level, it is just like the five-paragraph essay you may have been asked to write in high school. Yet, hopefully, by the end of this book, you will come to see this structure as clear, precise, and intuitively understandable.

## THE DISSERTATION TIMELINE

My doctoral students may be happy to see the entire process explained from start to finish, but they are still not satisfied; they still ask the truly uppermost question on their minds: how long is this going to take? For, in

**Figure 2.2** The Structure of a Five-Chapter Dissertation

| Chapter 1 Introduction | Chapter 2 Literature Review | Chapter 3 Methodology | Chapter 4 Findings | Chapter 5 Conclusions |
|---|---|---|---|---|
| What is the "big picture," and how will your research fit into it? | What does the research say? | How will you do it? | What did you find? | What are the conclusions, implications, and recommendations? |

the background of all worries about the doctoral process, is the realization that far too many doctoral students take far too long to finish. Stories of dissertations dragging on for years and years are legion. No matter how much we may want to say that we won't be like that, there is always a nagging doubt.

It is important to realize that there is no single timeline to a dissertation. There are, instead, lots and lots of mini-timelines. Think of it as a birth. When an expectant mother is told that her baby will be born in nine months, the date can feel deeply abstract and distant no matter how exciting or nerve-wracking. But as soon as the doctor explains the schedule of forthcoming visits—once a month the first six months with biweekly visits thereafter, with all types of blood testing, ultrasounds, measurements, etc.—it becomes pragmatically comprehensible and seemingly doable. Think of your dissertation as such, in some ways, as your next child.

Your dissertation "pregnancy," though, will not have the linear chronological development, since it is impossible to predict how long any given segment will truly take. Some doctoral students read or write much faster or slower than others; it may take one day or, alternatively, two months to gain permission to conduct the research in a specific school; your committee may ask for revisions five times, or, alternatively, not at all. Nevertheless, some basic guidelines can be provided simply based on the pragmatics of what needs to be accomplished in each stage: the preparation stage can take anywhere from three to six months; the research stage can take anywhere from three to twelve months; and the completion stage can take anywhere from one to three months.

The key variable at the preparation stage is how quickly you can convince your committee of the significance and viability of your research study. This can actually take quite a long time exactly because, as I suggested above, this is the most crucial step in your study. You may need to do significant amounts of background reading, write multiple drafts of your ideas, and test out multiple iterations of survey or interview questions. You may have done some of this already in your coursework, which may greatly speed up the process. But do not attempt to slide through this stage quickly and easily. The slow work done well at this stage will provide ample rewards later on in the process.

The culminating event at the preparation stage is the submission and defense of the dissertation proposal. While there are differences across institutions, most doctoral programs expect the dissertation proposal to be submitted to the committee a few weeks prior to the proposal defense (anywhere from two to six, depending on the institution). This gives the committee time to read and comment on the proposal as well as have the opportunity to ask for a revision if the proposal appears inadequate. You should also be aware that there are different "levels" of passing your proposal that may impact your timeline. Namely, if the committee believes that your proposal requires major changes, it may substantially slow down your immediate progress. Figure 2.3 provides the four options for passing a dissertation proposal in my doctoral program. While these levels are not universal, they provide a sense of the options the committee has concerning the dissertation proposal. Of most relevance at this point is to realize that your advisor may ask for major revisions before you can move to the next stage of the dissertation process.

**Figure 2.3**    Four Approval Options for the Dissertation Proposal

1. **Pass without modifications.** The student may immediately continue with the research process, which would include, if relevant, gaining the necessary IRB approval prior to commencing data collection.

2. **Pass with minor modifications.** The student may immediately continue the research process. This would include, if relevant, gaining the necessary IRB approval prior to commencing data collection, with the understanding that a modified dissertation proposal—based on feedback from the dissertation chair synthesized from the committee's feedback—should be submitted to the dissertation chair within fifteen days.

3. **Pass with major modifications.** The student must make the requested changes—based on feedback from the dissertation chair synthesized from the committee's feedback—before being able to continue with the research process. It is the responsibility of the dissertation chair to make the decision as to when the modified dissertation proposal has adequately addressed the requested changes; upon approval, the student can continue with the research process. This would include, if relevant, gaining the necessary IRB approval prior to commencing data collection.

4. **Fail.** The student must make the requested changes before being able to continue with the research process. Specifically, the modified dissertation proposal must be resubmitted to the entire committee, at which point the committee will again review it within twenty days and submit a decision to the dissertation chair.

Once a dissertation proposal has been approved, most students must then submit a research proposal to the Institutional Review Board at their institution. This committee, usually referred to as the IRB, is responsible for evaluating the ethical and legal status of the dissertation research and reviews any research that involves empirical data (as opposed to dissertations that are theoretical or historical and thus solely working with texts). Some dissertation research may be deemed unnecessary to review, such as already existing and public data sets. Other research, such as standardized surveys with adult populations, may go through a speeded-up, "expedited review." But many other times, especially when educational research involves children or sensitive topics (such as race and ethnicity, poverty, or self-esteem) may involve a more thorough review with—much like the dissertation-proposal stage—multiple requested revisions. The specific details of this process are discussed in Chapter 5 and detail how best to prepare for it. At this point, it is enough to realize that the dissertation proposal and IRB approval stages may take longer than expected.

Once your dissertation proposal and IRB (if necessary) are approved, you can begin the research phase of the process. The timeline now is in many ways dependent on how well your data collection proceeds. It may take time to conduct your interviews and transcribe all of them or send out and collect multiple rounds of surveys, enter the data, and analyze them. Especially if you are doing long-term fieldwork, your timeframe may span over a year rather than just weeks or even months.

Yet, I tell my doctoral students that the truly key variable at the research stage is not the collection and analysis of data, but writing it all up as a first draft. Data collection and analysis, even though it is viewed as the heart of the dissertation process, is in fact sometimes the easiest part of the process because it has been adequately prepared for in the dissertation proposal. In other words, you should already have the surveys created, the observation protocols ready, and the interview questions thought through. The hard part is putting it all together in a coherent and logical manner.

My doctoral students may easily have hundreds and hundreds of pages of data from interview transcriptions or statistical analysis printouts. They may have a dozen color-coded three-ring binders with the hundreds of research articles they have read which may be applicable to their own research. They may have dozens of pages of notes and ideas spread out over three or four different computer files. What takes time is combing through these data and writing up the relevant and most applicable parts. This is where doctoral students get writer's block because they finally have to synthesize their data and take a stance. They have to give voice to their research and ideas. Chapter 6 will help you conceptualize this and will assist you in working through this process.

Once you have sent a first draft to your advisor, you have entered the third and final stage of the process. You are nearing completion. You should, of course, be prepared that your advisor may ask you to collect more data since what you have may not be adequate to answering your research questions. But even if your advisor believes you have all of the necessary data, you are not done. Far from it. The key variable for the timeline at the completion stage is getting your advisor to approve the final draft that will be used for the defense. This is not as easy as it may sound. I, for example, usually go through four or five complete revisions with my own doctoral students, and this process and its goal are detailed in Chapter 6.

Suffice it to say, for now, that the final draft is all about a story that flows. Many doctoral students believe that their first draft is their final draft. No way. The stories that are truly well crafted, the ones that appear to flow so easily, are usually the hardest to write. It takes immense effort to make it appear effortless. You are understandably not writing a work of fiction that will win the Pulitzer Prize. But you want a coherent narrative. Moreover, your advisor will be checking to make sure that the conclusions are warranted, that you have answered the "so what?" question, and that you have situated your work within the literature, as well as a host of other points. But once your advisor accepts it, you're done. I know this sounds crazy, and it is explained more in Chapter 7. In any case, the hard part truly is getting to the final draft. The dissertation defense is the fun part.

## YOUR OWN TIMELINE AND BENCHMARKS

Let us now return to the very beginning, for you now need to "own" this process for yourself. Specifically, you now need to create your own timeline that actually matches your own schedule, work style, etc. Perhaps you have the summers off. Perhaps you write best in the early mornings. The key is to now—right now—begin to create space and time to focus on the dissertation. One of the best ways to do so is to create an actual timeline with specific dates and aligned goals.

I have created exactly such a template to help you with this process of developing a research timeline. The sections are expanded such that you can begin to see some of the key points within each stage. These points are not definitive; there are others that could have been added and perhaps one or two that you might not even do. The point, though, is that you can now use this template as a tool to set goals for yourself and even work with your dissertation chair to establish mutually agreed-upon timetables. Together, you can develop anticipated completion dates for each stage of the process and then use this write-up to keep track of your progress. As you move through each stage, it may be helpful to compare your original anticipated completion dates to your actual completion dates. You can always revise your timeline and goals depending on your particular situation and how this process unfolds.

| | Completion Date | |
|---|---|---|
| **Use This!** **Dissertation Research Timeline Template** | Anticipated | Actual |

**Preparation Stage**

1. Set up your research.
   a. Nurture academic relations
      (university, department, advisor, peers).
   b. Inform personal relations
      (work related, home related).

2. Focus your research.
   a. Conduct first and second round of literature review.
   b. Develop a methodological framework.
   c. Conduct informal pilot study.
   d. Submit preliminary write-up for advisor (prospectus).

3. Prepare for the dissertation proposal.
   a. Focus methodology.
   b. Focus second and third round of literature review.
   c. Develop necessary research tools and instruments.
   d. Conduct formal pilot study.
   e. Formalize dissertation committee (using updated prospectus).
   f. Create support networks.
   g. Create a timeline.

4. Submit dissertation proposal.

5. Submit IRB (upon approval of dissertation proposal).

**Research Stage**

6. Collect data.

7. Continue research and seek support.
   a. Complete third and fourth rounds of literature review.
   b. Participate in support networks.

8. Conduct data analysis.
   a. Additional data collection if recursive design.

9. Write first draft of dissertation.
   a. Develop comprehensive table of contents.
   b. Outline and draft chapters.

**Completion Stage**

10. Write complete draft and submit to advisor for initial approval.

11. Prepare for dissertation defense.
    a. Formalize dissertation defense date with committee and university.
    b. Write final dissertation draft.

12. Defend dissertation.

13. Finish up.
    a. Write abstract.
    b. Finalize revisions.
    c. Submit final version.

Still, no matter how well you believe you have set up your timeline, a dissertation (like all else in life) has ups and downs and ebbs and flows. Some aspects seem to go on forever while other components can be completed in one afternoon. So, which components in the research process really matter? What should a student focus on? What are the benchmarks that truly demonstrate progress?

As a dissertation chair, I tell my own students that I really only worry about three things: (1) passing the dissertation proposal, (2) collecting all of the data, and (3) making sure that the final conclusions align with the data gathered and original research questions asked. And, in reality, only the first two truly matter in regard to hurdles along the way and potential barriers to ultimately and successfully completing your dissertation. Your advisor will be able to help with the last part of aligning the data with conclusions. It is thus critical that you spend a little time setting very specific and doable benchmarks for yourself in regard to these two very important steps: passing the proposal and collecting your data.

Let me preface this discussion with another "big-picture" point: trust the process. All too often, doctoral students believe that they have to have every single stage of the dissertation process—and especially the dissertation proposal—picture perfect. They will revise and expand and refocus and cut and revise and expand . . . you get the idea. And while this is of course important, one must also realize that the dissertation proposal serves as a stage—an important stage, but nevertheless a stage—toward your real goal, which is the completion of your dissertation. So, when your dissertation chair tells you that you need to expand a section, do so. And when she tells you that it is ready to submit to your committee, submit it.

The key here is that no research is ever perfect. This includes proposals, dissertations, and even massive, federally funded studies. Instead, research has to be focused, transparent, meaningful, and valid. Moreover, all research is a work in progress. I cringe whenever I look back on my own dissertation; it is full of inconsistencies, generalizations, and tangents. There is of course some good research in it, else my advisor (and committee) would never have passed it. Yet, if I could do it again, it would be structured very, very differently. But now is now and then was then. When I did write it, I thought I was doing a great job. My advisor, now that I consider it, probably knew otherwise. But he, smart man that he was, helped me to focus on the areas that he could see I could modify and strengthen. The point here is not to lower your standards and expectations; it is to be realistic in what is and is not accomplishable. It is to realize that your advisor has a bigger picture of the process and knows what good research is and how to best present it.

The reason I focus on passing the proposal and collecting all of one's data is because those two benchmarks function as fulcrums in the dissertation process. Think of these as the tipping points on a playground seesaw that you, as an ant, are trying to climb up. The climb up the inclined plank is incredibly arduous and always appears to be sloped

## Hint! Roles and Responsibilities of Your Dissertation Chair

Your dissertation chair wears many hats, from cheerleader to critic. I have outlined below some of the key roles and responsibilities of a dissertation chair. This is not to say that a dissertation chair has to do each and every single one of them, much less do them perfectly. But she should try. A dissertation chair should . . .

**Read your work.** You will be writing many drafts of your dissertation. Your chair is responsible for carefully and thoroughly reading your work and providing helpful commentary and guidance to improve your writing. You should of course make use of writing centers, professional editors, and/or friends to help you improve your writing and edit your work. And you should not expect your advisor to read a draft and comment on it by the next day (though a week or two is realistic). But, it certainly is his job to read each and every page of your writing.

**Offer constructive criticism.** Your advisor should always be able to offer constructive criticism. There are, though, two parts to that phrase. Most students assume and expect that their chair will be constructive and helpful and supportive. But you should also realize that your advisor will be critical. No one's work is ever perfect, and the only way to improve is to get pushed to rethink and rephrase and reframe one's arguments and data and perspectives. That is most certainly your advisor's job, for there is really no one else who can and will push you that hard. Take such constructive criticism in the right sprit. It will only make your dissertation better.

**Be able to guide you when you are lost.** The point of a dissertation is not to wander around lost. If you don't know what to read or what the next step is, ask for help. Your advisor should know what your next step should be.

**Act as your ally and buffer with your committee.** A dissertation committee can be an unruly mess. One committee member wants you to do X and read Y. Another member wants you to do the opposite of X and read Z. What should you do? Ask your advisor. She must act as the mediator and synthesizer of the disparate (or complementary) ideas coming from your committee members. And when your committee members ask you at the proposal or final defense why you did or did not do X, she is the one who can quell the argument by pointing out that she made the decision as to how and why you should move forward as you did.

**Know if your topic is feasible and valuable.** You cannot know the literature before you begin. That is your advisor's job. He should know what has been done and who has done it. He should also know what your specific dissertation can contribute to what has already been done. If he says it is a feasible topic, you have to trust him. If he says it isn't, you have to trust him as well.

**Know the pitfalls of your approach.** Since, all too often, you are deep inside the issue, your advisor should be able to act as the "outsider" who can question why you are doing things one way rather than another. Where are the ethical pitfalls? What are the pragmatic limits? Where are the political challenges? Use your advisor as a support to see the blind spots that you many times cannot.

**Help you even after you have graduated.** A dissertation chair, they say, is for life. He should be willing to write you letters of recommendation after you have graduated, provide advice on how to publish your findings, and serve as an informal mentor as you move forward in your career. You, of course, could also choose to never see him or talk to him again. But if you want to, he should be willing to help.

uphill, forever. Yet, at some point—of which you were not aware but from above is obviously the midpoint of the seesaw—the seesaw shifts drastically, and all of a sudden you are racing down the incline at full speed. You had no clue when or why this change occurred, but you are deeply grateful for it. I, though, can tell you exactly when the change occurs (at least for the dissertation): it occurs exactly when you pass your proposal (and IRB) and again once you collect all of your data. At each of these moments, the process moves quickly and excitedly forward. After the passing of your proposal (and IRB), you can collect data as quickly as you want. Likewise, after the collection of all of your data, you can analyze and begin to write the first draft as fast as your brain can process the data and your fingers can type the manuscript. These are key and wonderful moments, and you should set them as your benchmarks.

I am not suggesting that all of this will be easy sailing. As I have mentioned, once a doctoral student has passed his proposal and IRB, he may feel deeply isolated. There is no more coursework, no more peers to be supported by, no more intense meetings with his advisor. He is, for all intents and purposes, in "ABD-land." It becomes hard to know when one is moving in the right direction or off on some crazy tangent. It may feel that you never have enough data or that what you have collected so far is not useful. Even after data collection is complete, there may be a feeling of exhaustion and uncertainty as to the next step. There may be fear that there is simply too much data to process or synthesize or examine.

Fortunately, all of these are manageable issues through simple and proven strategies: you can ask for help from friends and colleagues; you can seek out advice from colleagues who have gone through the process or from professors you have had in your courses; you can show your committee members the data and ask them if you are moving in the right direction. And you can always ask your dissertation advisor for help. That is his job.

A dissertation chair is—rightly or wrongly—the key person in your academic life for the duration of your dissertation. If she says you need to make revisions, you make them. If she says to not worry about an issue in the dissertation, don't worry about it. Again, whether rightly or wrongly, your dissertation chair has such authority because she is the one who can ultimately determine when your dissertation is ready to defend and will be the one who, in turn, defends you if and when other committee members question the viability of your dissertation. That is part of her job, as are a host of other roles and responsibilities (see the "hint" above). And (though this is hard to talk about), if your dissertation chair appears remiss in some of her duties, you should seriously consider changing advisors. Such an option is not to be taken lightly or done haphazardly. But even though this is never a "good" option, it may be better to go through the difficult process of changing advisors early in your dissertation process rather than go through the even more difficult process of keeping a dysfunctional advisor. Talk to your peers, to the graduate dean, or another appropriate administrator at your institution if you feel that you do indeed have a serious problem. A good dissertation chair is crucial to your success in creating and meeting the benchmarks you have just created as a means to gauge your dissertation progress.

## EMBRACING TECHNOLOGY

### THE TABLE OF CONTENTS AND REFERENCE LIST

It is difficult to remember how academic research and writing used to occur before the Internet, much less the computer. How did I gather all of my research? How did I rewrite and revise my work? How could anything have been accomplished without the spell-check and thesaurus feature? I am being just slightly flippant because while technological advances have both greatly expanded and simplified academic research, it is just as possible to write a poor dissertation with cutting-edge technology as with a quill pen. Technology in and of itself will not write your dissertation, but the prudent use of it may greatly simplify the process and save you lots and lots of time.

It is beyond the scope of this book to serve as primer on the role of technology in research. Suffice it to say that this can range from the mundane aspects of formatting charts and texts to cutting-edge research involving search engines, data mining, transcript analysis, and statistical analysis. Certain aspects of these issues are covered in Chapter 3 and 5, so for now, two more narrow and seemingly pedestrian means of using technology can nevertheless be immensely helpful: the table of contents and the reference list.

Even at the very beginning of the process, as I mentioned in the first chapter, it is already possible to create a detailed and almost comprehensive structure for your dissertation. This is your table of contents. Perhaps you may see this as one of the more mundane components of a dissertation, the seemingly detailed and tedious work of making things look right and formatted correctly. Yet, the table of contents is much more than this. It is a critical structure that allows you to begin to put some meat (and bones) on the still ethereal timeline and benchmarks you have begun developing.

A good table of contents provides a snapshot of the dissertation to the reader, displays a clear map of what each chapter contains, and offers an overview to the reader interested in jumping to particular sections. Moreover, and to put it in the negative phrasing, a poor (or worse, inaccurate) table of contents demonstrates (to the reader, at least) a lack of attention to detail, which is a sure sign of more problems to come. A good table of contents will thus function as a structure to your forward progress.

I have created a table of contents template that you can use as the initial basis for your particular dissertation topic. I have structured the template to show that a dissertation proposal is structured very similarly to the final dissertation. While the actual content will change dramatically (no, you can't just cut and paste from the proposal to the dissertation and be done; sorry), the structure from the proposal to the final dissertation remains the same. All that changes in the final dissertation is the addition of data and conclusions and the filling in of minor gaps in the first chapters that cannot be done before data are collected and conclusions developed.

It should be noted that there will be distinct differences between a qualitative and quantitative dissertation. The differences can be as subtle as presuming different notions of, and thus discussions about, what constitutes an appropriate research tool. (That is in quantitative research, the research instrument must be shown to be both valid and reliable; in qualitative research, the researcher is often the "research instrument.") Or, it can be as obvious as a qualitative dissertation having six chapters whereas a quantitative dissertation may have four chapters.

In either case, the point

---

## Hint! Creating an Automated Table of Contents

It is very simple to create an automated table of contents. An automated table of contents allows you to automatically make updates throughout the document, whether this means adding, deleting, or modifying chapters, sections, and subsections. Here's how to do it (I focus here solely on MSWord 2007 for PCs):

1. With your cursor at the beginning of the document, click on the "References" tab and then click on "Table of Contents" on the very left-hand side of the bar. This will open up multiple formatting options for how you want the table of contents to look. Choose one.

2. This sets up the table of contents template. You can now either just start typing or use your already existing draft to create chapters, sections, and subsections. To create a section, for example, just type it in (e.g., "Historical Context of School Reform in California"), highlight it, and click on the pull-down tab "Add Text" (to the right of the table of contents button). Set up the section as a "level 2." Chapter titles are usually "level 1," sections are "level 2," and subsections are "level 3." Dissertations don't usually go deeper than the third level (but ask your advisor for specifics).

3. Click on the "Update Table" button (below the "Add Text" button) and the program will automatically put this section title and the corresponding page number in your table of contents. Make sure to periodically click this update button so that your table of contents stays current.

---

is simply that you should use this template as a starting point for your own dissertation. While the detail for possible sections is fairly comprehensible, you may have to add additional sections specific to your study or not use others that have no relevance to your particular dissertation. Don't presume that just because a section is listed in the template, you have to write about it. Every dissertation will have slight nuances, and every dissertation chair will have her particular preferences. Work with your dissertation chair to modify and individualize this template for your own work.

| Use This!  Table of Contents Template | |
| --- | --- |
| Dissertation Proposal | Final Dissertation |
| • Front Matter<br><br>   o Title page<br>   o Table of contents<br>   o List of tables (only if tables used)<br>   o List of figures (only if figures used) | • Front Matter<br><br>   o Signature page<br>   o Title page<br>   o Copyright page (not required)<br>   o Acknowledgements (not required)<br>   o Dedication (not required)<br>   o Abstract<br>   o Table of contents<br>   o List of tables (only if tables are used)<br>   o List of figures (only if figures are used) |
| • Introduction<br><br>   o Statement of the problem<br>   o Research questions<br>   o Purpose and significance of study<br>   o Local context<br>   o Conceptual framework<br>   o Limitations of study<br>   o Background and role of researcher<br>   o Definition of relevant terms<br>   o Organization of the study | • Chapter 1: Introduction<br><br>   o Statement of the problem<br>   o Research questions<br>   o Purpose and significance of study<br>   o Local context<br>   o Conceptual framework<br>   o Limitations of study<br>   o Summary of findings<br>   o Background and role of researcher<br>   o Definition of relevant terms<br>   o Organization of the study |
| • Literature Review<br><br>   o Introduction<br>   o Theoretical framework<br>   o Review of literature strand 1, 2, 3, etc.<br>   o Summary and implications of literature review | • Chapter 2: Literature Review<br><br>   o Introduction<br>   o Theoretical framework<br>   o Review of literature strand 1, 2, 3, etc.<br>   o Summary and implications of literature review |
| • Methodology<br><br>   o Research questions<br>   o Research design<br>   o Setting<br>   o Overall and sample populations<br>   o Access to site (gaining access and entry, obtaining participant participation, exiting, etc.)<br>   o Value of specific qualitative methodology<br>   o Instrumentation | • Chapter 3: Methodology<br><br>   o Research questions<br>   o Research design<br>   o Setting<br>   o Overall and Sample Populations<br>   o Access to site (gaining access and entry, obtaining participant participation, exiting, etc.)<br>   o Value of specific methodology<br>   o Instrumentation (reliability and validity) |

| Dissertation Proposal | Final Dissertation |
|---|---|
| <ul><li>Reliability and validity</li><li>Data collection procedures</li><li>Data analysis procedures</li><li>Validity of interpretation (applicability, consistency, trustworthiness)</li><li>Limitations and delimitations</li><li>Ethical considerations</li></ul> | <ul><li>Data collection procedures</li><li>Data analysis procedures</li><li>Validity of interpretation (applicability, consistency, trustworthiness)</li><li>Limitations and delimitations</li><li>Ethical considerations</li></ul><br>• Chapter 4: Findings<ul><li>Data description</li><li>Data analysis<ul><li>Results for total sample, subsample 1, subsample 2, across subsamples, etc.</li><li>Results vis-à-vis initial research questions</li></ul></li></ul><br>• Chapter 5: Discussion, Conclusions, and Implications<ul><li>Discussion of findings<ul><li>Subsections for findings for each specific research questions</li></ul></li><li>Limitations of findings</li><li>Researcher comments (e.g., personal reflections on research methodology; reflections on impact on research site/individuals)</li><li>Relationship of findings to previous literature</li><li>Implications for future practice in local context</li><li>Implications for future research</li></ul> |
| <ul><li>Reference List</li><li>Appendices<ul><li>IRB forms (e.g., informed consent forms)</li><li>Timeline</li><li>Instrumentation</li></ul></li></ul> | <ul><li>Reference List</li><li>Appendices<ul><li>IRB forms (e.g., informed consent forms)</li><li>Instrumentation</li></ul></li></ul><br>• Vita (not required) |

Much like the table of contents structures the dissertation from the very beginning, the reference list can be seen as the final bookend to this structure. Namely, the reference list functions as the repository of all of the citations throughout the dissertation. Whether this is thirty or three hundred, the reference list must also reflect the same attention to detail and consistency as the table of contents.

In some ways, this is extremely easy. The reference list is highly formulaic, with strict formatting rules and guidelines. (That is every in-text citation in the body of your dissertation should be listed in alphabetical order in the reference list; and, vice versa, every citation in the reference list should be found somewhere in the dissertation.) Likewise, the content of each citation is repetitive. Every journal article, for example, should have specific information, such as the volume number, page numbers, and all author names. The specific citation style you use (whether it is APA, MLA, Turabian, or another popular style) has very specific guidelines regarding punctuation, capitalization, italics, and a myriad of other details. What could be so hard?

In one respect, a reference list isn't hard so much as it may be time consuming and repetitive. Yet, on the other hand, it is deeply inefficient to manually type in each and every single reference and confirm that it matches the specific citation style required by your institution. One inefficiency lies in the fact that there really is no single reference list; you may have a list of texts that you have read but did not cite, other texts that are relevant for a conference paper you are writing but are tangential to the dissertation, and even other texts that you plan on using but have not yet read. It is inefficient to retype or crosscheck across multiple reference lists. Another inefficiency lies in the fact that citation style guidelines are complex: How do you handle the citation of Web sites, especially those that are no longer available? How do you differentiate between a magazine article, newspaper article, and an internal newsletter? Does the edition of the book matter? To research and check the minutia of hundreds of references is a daunting undertaking.

I thus highly recommend, just like with the table of contents, that you embrace technology to greatly simplify your life and save untold hours of time and frustration. There is a wide variety of citation software—some free, others fairly expensive, most computer based, but more and more available as Web based—that will create the reference list for you in whatever style you choose. You can enter the information yourself or, much more preferred, use the software to search in multiple Web-based public databases to find and download the citations you need into a personalized database. Once in the database, it is extremely easy to organize, manipulate, and reformat citations to suit your particular needs and citation style. And while it may take you several hours to become familiar with and begin to productively use such software, the hours spent learning this at the beginning will save you tenfold over the course of the dissertation process.

The table of contents and reference list are thus ideal examples of the value of using task-specific software to simplify your dissertation process. Realize that you will be doing some things over and over and over again during your dissertation. As such, it is critical that you automate as much of these tasks as possible. Likewise, there are an immense number of software packages that can help you, for example, organize your thoughts, structure projects, display complex relationships, keep notes and analyze them for patterns, and coordinate your time-management priorities. The key is to find what works with your strengths and patterns and start using such tools earlier rather than later. The dissertation process is long, and there is no need to make it any longer.

## STRUCTURING YOUR LIFE AS A DOCTORAL STUDENT

The roadmap I have been discussing so far has been about your dissertation. Let's now talk about you. For you too need a roadmap. You too need to begin to figure out how to structure your life, think about the process ahead, and understand what you have gotten yourself into and how to think about your own role. Let me, then, offer a few concluding thoughts about how to move forward as a doctoral student at the dissertation stage.

One of the first points I make to my doctoral students is that they have to learn to say no. Doctoral students are by definition a self-selected population. You would not have gotten as far as you have in your career and your education if you had not had intense motivation and ambition. People who enjoy coming home early from work and lounging on their deck chairs don't pursue a doctoral degree. You are successful exactly because you are driven; to be frank, you probably have more than a little chutzpah. Only about one in three individuals in the United States has a bachelor's degree and less than 2 percent of those with bachelor's degrees ever complete their doctorates (Planty et al., 2008). Yet, here you are, presumptuous enough to think you can complete your doctorate. That says something about you.

What it says is that you don't know how to say no. You tackle every challenge that crosses your desk; you join every committee and end up as the leader who writes the report; you spend that extra hour and extra day preparing so the lesson is not just good, but great. What I suggest to my doctoral students is that they can't do this any longer—or at least not if they want to finish the dissertation.

This is a hard pill to swallow. They have gotten where they are exactly because they have been able to juggle everything at the same time. They think that perhaps they can do this balancing act just one more time with the dissertation. They usually can't. And the reason that they can't is that doing a dissertation is different from being on an extra committee or doing an extra class prep. Doing a dissertation requires concentrated time to read, think, and write. This does not mean it is "harder" than what you are now doing. It is simply different. This difference needs to be respected and attended to in order to be successful at it. This difference necessitates that you are able to close your door or find a quiet spot at the library and not be disturbed for one or two or three hours. A day. Every day. Every week. Every month. Until you're done. So, I tell my students that they have to learn to say no to that extra class or committee or book club or big brother project or whatever. It is not forever that you have to pull away from other responsibilities—just until you're finished, else you'll never finish.

A second major point is that you need to learn to develop thick skin. Our culture in general, and our schools and workplaces in specific, are not very good at giving and receiving criticism. We all too often hide behind euphemisms ("good try") and seemingly "objective" grading ("that was a B+ paper"). That's not how it works at the doctoral level. The dissertation process is all about realizing, and embracing, how much you actually don't know or understand.

It is, in fact, your professors' and advisor's job to help you along this path of realization. This is what comes to be termed your limitations and delimitations in your dissertation: all of the stuff that you won't cover and that can't be covered in your research. But at the beginning of the process, it may feel simply like people are telling you that you are dumb: no, you won't be able cover gender variation; and, no, you won't be able to link this to how they do it at the high school level; and, no, I really don't think four months of fieldwork is enough to measure that subtle an issue; and, no, your process is actually highly biased toward certain socioeconomic groups; and, no, this doesn't really apply outside of your specific context. And by the way, your advisor will ask, Did you really think about this or that or this? And have you yet read him or her or him? You probably should. And, oh yes, are you really sure you meant what you wrote on page 17? How does that square with what you wrote on page 35? You probably should rethink and thus rewrite one or the other.

This kind of criticism—probing, deep, and detailed—is a wonderful thing. It reveals your assumptions and sheds light on the muddiness of your thinking. It clarifies the implications of your arguments and helps you to make connections that were unclear before. It, simply put, stretches the boundaries of your understanding and makes you a more careful thinker and writer. And that is a good thing. But only once you get used to it. Accepting criticism in a productive way is a learned habit and difficult to do. Yet, always remember that it is done in your best interest and in good faith. The culture of the academy is about questioning and expanding knowledge, and you are now a part of it. Embrace it, for it is the only way that you will be able to truly focus (and thus complete) your research.

# 3

## *Focusing Your Research*

Ⅰt is almost silly to point out that a dissertation is about a specific topic. Yet, while this may sound obvious, it is actually immensely difficult to articulate a focused, specific, and doable dissertation topic. The doctoral students in my program come in with dissertation ideas that are marvelous and important and complex . . . and undoable. They are undoable because rather than just one idea, they are really three or four or even five ideas. As I tell each cohort of students again and again, they need to focus. A dissertation is in this regard much like gardening—the profusion of ancillary ideas may kill off the main growth. Rather than letting a thousand ideas bloom, the key is to prune and weed and allow the central idea to truly blossom.

Topics such as "the dropout problem of at-risk youth" or "the future of district school-choice plans" are excellent starting points for further investigation and narrowing; they are not, though, dissertation topics. A dissertation topic is a highly bounded question, one that is contained to a very specific event, idea, or context. Figure 3.1 shows some of the dissertations that I have chaired or been a committee member on.

But the questions remain: How do you know when a topic is too broad? When is a question too vague or an idea too abstract? At one level, this is something that your dissertation advisor will ultimately decide. She will be the one guiding and supporting your study, and, as such, she has final say on when a topic is well-articulated and focused. Yet, it will save you and your dissertation advisor a lot of time and effort if you can begin

| Figure 3.1 | Examples of Dissertation Titles |
|---|---|

A good dissertation is a focused dissertation. Note how each of these dissertation titles offers an important and bounded research focus with a very clear problem to be solved.

- Race and Referrals: Teacher Attitudes, Culturally Relevant Teaching, and the Special Education Referrals of African American Males
- Nontraditional Student Success: A Systematic Approach to Adult-Student Retention Planning for a Two-Year Postsecondary Institution
- Building Racial Harmony: A Study of Racial Identity, Culture, and Prejudice in an Urban High School
- Multidimensional Classrooms: Developing a Comprehensive Research Base for Holistic Teaching and Learning
- Nonnegotiable Expectations: A Program Evaluation of the Transformation of East Technical High School
- Making a Difference in Afterschool Programs: A Study of Research-Based Promising Practices and Model Programs
- Career Decisions: The Impact of Mentoring on Novice Teachers
- Expanding Success: Scaling Up School-Dropout Prevention in Four Public Alternative High Schools

the process yourself, formulating and focusing your idea with but a few modifications (rather than countless revisions) to articulate a dissertation topic that is a clear and manageable project. This chapter takes you through this step-by-step process, from articulating and focusing your topic to turning it into a tentative research question and dissertation title. This, in turn, will help you (illustrated in Chapter 4) determine a theoretical framework, conduct a literature review, and choose a research design and methodology. In a sense, this stage in the process is highly paradoxical. You must articulate your project as succinctly and clearly as possible before you have even figured out exactly what you are going to do or how to do it. Nevertheless, you must trust the process, as the iterative nature of formulating and revising your dissertation idea is crucial to narrowing and thus clarifying your research.

Here is an analogy to begin to think about how to focus your dissertation idea. Imagine if you told your friends that you were heading off to Rio de Janeiro without a map: "Oh, I'll just drive south and ask people along the way." While you might, in fact, actually get there at some point, it would be a meandering and difficult process. This is even an overly optimistic example because you actually already have a specific goal in mind. Attempting to write an unfocused dissertation is, in many ways, even more analogous to saying something like, "In the next year, I want to get smarter." This is a nice idea, but extremely vague. What do you want to get smarter about? What resources do you have to accomplish this goal? How will you know if you have succeeded?

The need to focus, and do so from the very beginning, is an extremely difficult and frustrating lesson for the doctoral student to learn; one cannot "wing" a dissertation. Even if you could, your dissertation committee wouldn't let you. A dissertation is a concentrated and concerted focus on a very detailed and specific issue, be it the value of a new fourth-grade reading intervention or the pitfalls of an organizational change model for restructuring a large urban high school into several small, autonomous schools of choice.

This is the rub of the problem. The completion of a dissertation in a timely fashion is about setting very narrow and defined goals. But most experienced educators—at the classroom, district, or state level—really want to change the world. They want to find the perfect pedagogical strategy, or modify the next management initiative that will overcome midlevel bureaucratic inertia, or rewrite the state's math curriculum to overcome the achievement gap.

This mind-set, sadly, is the first thing that has to be thrown out. A dissertation is a huge, important, life-altering experience. But it will not change the world. It will not change your classroom, or school, or school district. What you ultimately do with your dissertation research might, in fact, accomplish some of these things. But your dissertation won't. While I hate to tell you this, few will really even bother to read your dissertation. Your dissertation advisor certainly will. Your dissertation committee will most likely read all of it as well. Your mother might skim parts of it. But after that, sorry.

The point here is not to make fun of or discourage you. It is rather to be very clear that your task is to engage in an intense and concentrated analysis of a very focused and specific topic. It is an opportunity to become an expert on a very small part of a huge field of education. A dissertation is not about inventing or reinventing or even revising the wheel. It is instead, to continue the analogy, about using the wheels others have created to better understand an educational issue important to you. It is, to borrow an oft-used yet very apt cliché, about standing on the shoulders of others.

In many ways, as well, the dissertation is as much about the process undertaken as the product achieved. When done well, a dissertation will have allowed you to practice developing a clear and answerable question, research in-depth the literature available, analyze and apply such literature, conduct and analyze empirical research, and, ultimately, draw supportable and relevant conclusions from such research—all on a single, specific topic. Once you can do such work on any single topic, you can do it on any topic. This is why I often talk about the dissertation as a pilot project. Whereas most of my doctoral students see the dissertation as the culminating endpoint of their educational goals, I tell them just the opposite: your dissertation is the beginning of your newly developed role as a practitioner scholar. This is discussed in much more detail in Chapter 7; for now, be clear that the first and most crucial step is your need to realize that you are going to focus all of your energy and effort on a single, specific issue. Put simply, if you can't articulate your topic or a draft of the idea in one or two sentences by the end of this chapter, you won't be able to adequately research or write about it either. Take the time, then, to do the activities and exercises that follow as a way to focus and define your dissertation topic.

## ARTICULATING A TOPIC IN "ACADEMIC-SPEAK"

Assuming that you already have an idea for your dissertation, it is not a problem if your idea is still somewhat vague, if you have several different versions of it, or even if you are not sure that you have thought about it in the right way. The key is that you have an idea to work with that is important to you. This point—that the idea is one that you care passionately about—will serve as a touchstone throughout your dissertation process. As you will shortly see, the dissertation focus you finally end up with may look drastically different than the one you originally thought you were going to do. In many cases, the original idea morphs so many times that doctoral students are bewildered at the transformation, wondering, "Is this what I really wanted to work on?" With this in mind, you must begin with a firm conviction that, irrespective of how an idea may be modified, it is still the issue you care about and want to spend the next year or so of your life investigating.

But an idea does not a dissertation make. The first step is that you must be able to articulate your idea within the language of educational research, which is unfortunately all too often derisively termed "academic-speak" because of its seemingly opaque and incomprehensible jargon. This is often a frustrating task, and you will not be the first one to question the relevance of this endeavor. You have an idea and a passion—let's say it's helping at-risk students succeed—but most educational literature works with a very different nomenclature that seems far removed from your practitioner's day-to-day usage and reality and seems to have even less of an impact.

Don't be dismayed. The key insight to come to accept is that education is an immensely difficult endeavor to research. Schooling is what researchers term a "wicked problem" because there are so many variables interacting with each other, at multiple levels, and in multiple ways. To be able to say anything about education with any sense of surety requires that the research question be extremely focused and analytically clear. Good research cannot simply talk about someone being a "good teacher" because they "connect" with the kids. Such ideas have to be deeply examined on a host of levels to be able to articulate one's real goals and meaning with any clarity. It doesn't matter whether you are sending out surveys, conducting interviews, or observing classrooms; you have to be able to articulate what you are examining. This is why you must master a new vocabulary.

You do not have to do this on your own starting from scratch. In fact, almost all of the work has already been done for you. You just need to know where to look and make use of it in the right way. I thus suggest that the first step is to begin to compile a linked list of what are known as "descriptors" (or "subject descriptors") on your idea; I think of this as your "academic word bank" that will serve as the basis for developing and honing your research questions and dissertation title. Use the following activity to help you create your own.

## TRY THIS! DEVELOPING YOUR ACADEMIC WORD BANK

The best place to start your academic word bank is in ERIC (which stands for the Education Resources Information Center and can be found online at http://www.eric.ed.gov), a U.S. Department of Education resource that has the world's largest database of education-related literature. Go to the ERIC homepage and follow these four steps:

1. **Do a quick search.** Take your idea—which is really, in the language of educational research, just a "keyword"—and enter it into the "Search Term" box. At this point, it doesn't really matter if you are doing a search by "keyword" or "subject" or "descriptor" or an overall search. Your search should produce a list that could be as short as ten or as long as 10,000 publications. If your search comes up with less than ten publications, just try a different keyword.

2. **Choose any interesting publication.** Scroll down the generated list and simply click on any book or article that has an appealing title. Don't read the whole thing! All you care about at this point is the descriptor (often also termed "subject" or "subject descriptor" in other catalogs).

3. **Write down the relevant descriptors.** A publication may have just a few descriptors or as many as twenty or so. Write down the ones that seem interesting and important to your research interest. You have just started your word bank.

4. **Keep searching.** Return to your original search list and keep looking for other relevant titles. Remember, the key at this point is to gather as many descriptors as possible, not to read the documents you find. That's for later. There are also, by the way, lots of other ways to continue searching. You can, for example, click on any of the descriptors of a publication, which will link you to another list of publications that have that same descriptor; you can also use the built-in thesaurus in ERIC (find the "thesaurus" tab). You can also start a brand new search to see what else may turn up. Either way, keep searching until you have at least fifty relevant descriptors in your word bank.

You can now use this "academic word bank" of terms to describe and research your idea. While this list will be modified over time as you focus and tighten your research focus, it is an excellent first step in learning the new language of educational research. (It will also, as I will shortly show, serve as the basis for your research question and dissertation title.)

To give you an example of this process, I decided to create an academic word bank of my initial interest for "at-risk students." I typed this term into the ERIC search engine and came up with 10,226 publications. I then somewhat randomly chose an article titled "Predictors of Categorical At-Risk High School Dropouts" published in 2007 in the *Journal of Counseling & Development*. The descriptors for this article included the following terms: High Risk Students, Dropouts, Grade Point Average, Dropout Rate, Low Income, Socioeconomic Status, Statistical Analysis, Longitudinal Studies, and High School Students. Some of these terms related to my interest; others didn't. I then started to compile a list using these descriptors, going back to the main search list, and linking across the ERIC database through other descriptors that seemed relevant. Figure 3.2 provides a sample of the word bank I created.

**Figure 3.2**   Sample Academic Word Bank

My search in ERIC using the initial keyword of "at-risk students" resulted in literally thousands of publications and descriptors. Ultimately, I chose about fifty terms that seemed relevant to my general research topic and organized them around three broad categories. All of the terms listed below are directly from the ERIC database.

1. High Risk Students → Academic Failure; Attitude Measures; Dropout Rate; Dropout Research; Dropouts; Educational Attainment; English (Second Language); Hispanic Americans; Migrant Education; Minority Groups; Peer Influence; Psychological Patterns; Student Attitudes; Student Diversity; Student Motivation

2. Educational Improvement → College Preparation; Cultural Awareness; Dropout Prevention; Dropout Programs; Educational Environment; Experiential Learning; Heterogeneous Grouping; Multicultural Textbooks; Multilingualism; Nontraditional Education; Parent School Relationship; School Holding Power; Small Classes; Social Integration; Student Diversity; Teacher Education Programs; Teacher Student Relationship

3. Justice → Action Research; Biculturalism; Bilingual Education; Black Studies; Critical Theory; Cross Cultural Studies; Cultural Context; Cultural Differences; Cultural Pluralism; Culturally Appropriate Education; Culturally Relevant Education; Culturally Responsive Education; Culture Based Curriculum; Culture Fair Tests; Diversity; Ethnic Groups; Ethnicity; Multicultural Education; Power Structure; Student Centered Curriculum

This process may take a while and you may not really know where you are going or why you are choosing what you are choosing. That's fine. At this point, you are simply beginning to focus your ideas and gain a sense of the academic nomenclature used to talk about the issues you care about. Hopefully, as you continue this search process, you will become more adept at understanding how some descriptors relate to others, and how, in turn, such descriptors are linked to particular publications and research foci. This dialectical process—moving back and forth between your own research interests and the academic terminology used to describe such research—should help you begin to actually understand such "jargon" as meaningful and relevant. You now, to return to the analogy of driving to Rio de Janeiro, have a lot of road signs that point toward South America. The next step is to tighten the research focus to not just a continent, but the actual country of Brazil.

## NARROWING YOUR TOPIC

It is around this stage that a doctoral student begins to feel very, very lost. You came into your doctoral program with an idea for what you wanted to do. You may have even had a very specific intervention or idea that you wanted to pursue. But now, after some searching, your topic seems completely out of reach. There are literally dozens of keywords, and thus directions, which all seem relevant and important. And, behind each keyword are dozens of other keywords. Each keyword, in turn, links to dozens (if not hundreds) of publications with their own keywords. Argh!

It is at this stage that two points must be clearly stated, and these will be repeated in one form or another throughout this book. First, get used to it. All of us as educational scholars feel, to a smaller or greater extent, overwhelmed by the amount of research—both old and new—that we must master. Just as life is not lived in separate and nonoverlapping boxes, neither is educational research. Everything is in one respect or another related. So, as soon as I feel competent in, for example, project-based science instruction, I must confront the fact that I now need to better understand how this type of instruction may relate to differences in students' learning styles across racial, ethnic, and gender groupings.

This is why a dissertation is a highly focused and limited project. You are going to become an expert in and master a body of knowledge about a very little slice of an immensely huge pie. It is of course useful and important to taste different parts of the pie. But there is absolutely no way that you can even come close to consuming the whole pie or even a large slice of it. (That would be one massive stomachache and headache.) And there is in fact absolutely nothing wrong with that. You will not be a failure because you did not become an expert in "at-risk students." That takes an entire career. In fact, the broader you want your expertise

## Hint! Writing Your Other Dissertation Next Time

Tightening your research focus can be an excruciating process. You want to do everything. You want to know about and research all of the important topics and issues that you are coming across and reading about. Every time you make a decision to cut something, it feels like you are throwing away a part of yourself. But don't despair. You need to keep in mind two important things.

First, the process of pruning ideas is critical to the ultimate success of your dissertation. The more you attempt to cover at this stage, the harder it will be as you move forward. The additional work later on—in terms of reading and gathering and analyzing data—becomes exponential, not linear, with each topic you want to hold onto. The better the focus at this point, the stronger the dissertation.

Second, there is a life after the dissertation. Many educators continue to write about and speak about their research after they have defended their dissertation. This may take the form of consulting, presenting at conferences, or publishing articles and books for general or expert audiences. Additionally, the dissertation research often reveals new and unseen avenues for future exploration. You don't have to do it all at once.

As such, every time you cut an idea that you just "have to" do, just write it down on a list (that will get ever longer) that you can return to when you're done. Remember, the key is to finish this dissertation. You can do another one at another time.

to be, the greater the likelihood that you will fail. While this may seem counterintuitive at first, it is part and parcel of educational research. This is not to suggest that you focus your research on a grain of sand, but neither should you focus on the whole beach.

Second, remember your passion. You entered your doctoral program with a vision (however vague) of what you wanted to study. You must now return to that vision to remind yourself that while it may be important to study the entire panoply of issues surrounding at-risk students, what you really care about is, for example, developing structures and practices to support minority students' postsecondary educational aspirations. And even more specifically, your vision arises within the context of your particular educational and professional background.

This is not to say that the dissertation should be about you. It shouldn't. But your experiences must serve as the backdrop and impetus for this dissertation, because a dissertation does not write itself. You—an individual with a particular history and passion—write it. If I were discussing your aspirations to be in a traditional PhD program that stretched out over half a decade or more and that led you directly toward a full-time faculty position in higher education, I might offer different advice. But you are not in your program to become an academic scholar. You are attempting to link theory and practice in order to make a difference. You are a practitioner scholar using this dissertation as a stepping-stone to improve your classroom, your district, your state, or your disciplinary field. Your experience thus matters; it will help you cut out many other ideas and issues and begin to focus on a very specific issue.

To put this concretely into numbers, you should be able to cut the number of terms in your word bank in half just by remembering the reason you entered your doctoral program in the first place. In other words, while many of the topics and ideas in your word bank may seem interesting and even important, they probably do not directly relate to your true research interest. So, just cut them out. Then, take a little time to think carefully and honestly about the remaining topics and realize that probably half of the remaining descriptors—while all related and critical—may not be as relevant as some others. This may take a while. You may need to go back into ERIC and look again at the publications that have such descriptors; you may read the abstracts or even skim the articles; you may conduct multiple searches using such keywords by themselves or in combination. But the end result should be—through reminding yourself of your passions, experiences, and background—that you are able to refine the original list of fifty or so descriptors and be left with a list of a dozen or so. (By the way, don't despair about "losing" those other seemingly critical descriptors; you can write your other dissertation next time!)

You are now left with a word bank of a dozen or so descriptors that are a much better indicator of your research interest. Even so, this may seem like a lot, for each descriptor is linked to fifteen or so other descriptors. And each of those descriptors may link to anywhere between ten and a hundred articles on that topic. Yikes! When put that way, you may be asking yourself, am I in any way better off than when I began? The short and sweet answer is "yes."

What you have just accomplished, however tentatively, is to take an amorphous and vague idea and transform it into an analytically distinct set of topics. This set of topics may still be immensely huge at this stage. But it is now a concrete, stable, and defined set of topics and subtopics. You have moved from "dissertation-as-a-blob" to "dissertation-as-path" through a scaffolded pyramid (see Figure 3.3). This reorientation ultimately allows you—through the choosing of a theoretical framework and through multiple literature-review stages—to systematically cut sections of the pyramid that are not essential to your topic until you are left with a very focused and singular path to your specific research question.

It is strategically critical to understand this process of cutting away at your "pyramid" through a series of decision-making steps. An idea at the "blob" stage has no boundaries or sense of alternatives. If asked whether your passion for supporting at-risk students involved issues of culturally relevant pedagogy (or enhanced self-esteem or the problems of negative peer-group influences or whatever), you would probably have said "of course" without exactly knowing how they all related to each other. Even more problematically, if you had said "no" and cut peer groups out of the topic, you might not have been really sure about what you were cutting. A

**Figure 3.3**   Moving From a "Dissertation-as-Blob" to a "Dissertation-as-Path"

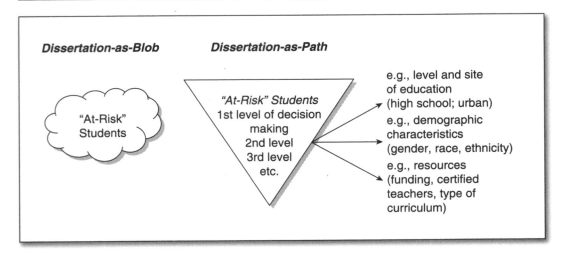

scaffolded pyramid of decision-making levels solves all of these problems by allowing you to make explicit choices and know exactly what is being chosen at each successive level.

Staying with the example of at-risk students, I might first decide the educational level and geographic locale I will be focusing on. Let's say I was a science teacher at an urban high school. I would thus decide to focus on risk factors for high school students in urban, under-resourced schools. I have just narrowed and focused my topic at the first decision-making level. I might then need to make additional decisions about whether my focus would differentiate between girls and boys and about whether I would take into account ethnic and racial groups. At this second level, I have just set up a whole set of decision-making points that, step-by-step and decision-by-decision, will help me to focus my topic. An initial ERIC search as well as other readings may have shown me the importance of academically rigorous hands-on learning as a means to engage at-risk youth. I might, as such, focus on how a hands-on curriculum in high-school science may positively impact girls traditionally at risk for dropping out of school.

Such step-by-step decision making allows you to tentatively develop and focus your dissertation idea. All of those other topics in your academic word bank—peer influences, small class sizes, English language learners, teacher–student relations—may still be important, but they no longer have direct and immediate relevance to your dissertation research. You may (and should) modify this decision-making process tomorrow or next week or next month and reintroduce some of these issues back into your dissertation, but for now, you have, however tentatively, taken your first steps down the path of focusing and narrowing your dissertation research.

What you are really doing as you go about cutting away at your dissertation idea is what can be thought of as "disaggregating the idea." Disaggregation is simply defined as the splitting apart of a specific whole; while we intuitively do this all the time in our daily lives, it is a difficult yet critical part of refining your dissertation idea, irrespective of whether you will be doing a quantitatively or qualitatively focused dissertation. This is because I, as the researcher, need to understand for myself how multiple complex variables interact and relate to each other. I may focus on a specific variable such as girls' self-esteem in science class through surveys and interviews, or I may want to naturalistically observe how girls' interaction patterns in a science classroom shape their sense of self with their peers and parents. In either case, I need to clarify for myself and for the research what I will be focusing on since I cannot focus on everything and anything.

While the actual disaggregation of data is a highly complex statistical process, all of us have run across this concept (and do it all the time) when we talk and hear about the election process. In the midst of the 2008 presidential election, for example, political pundits constantly worried about which candidate would capture the critical "swing voters" of Hispanics, "soccer moms," white males, or whichever demographic group happened to appear key in the moment. When Barack Obama won a key state in the primaries, exit polls would immediately focus on whether he was able to carry older white women or the college-educated evangelical vote. This polling was carefully and critically realizing that there is not a single voting bloc. Each demographic—women, whites, those older than age 55—was its own constituency, and the polling data had to analyze, combine, and recombine different permutations to get at seemingly meaningful results.

This is a critical process and you should try it now with your own dissertation research. You have to be able to take your idea and differentiate whether your issue is relevant, for example, across all grade levels or only at the elementary school level. Put otherwise, each decision along the path is the disaggregation of your idea such that there is a clear and coherent understanding of what exactly you will be examining in your dissertation. Presidential candidates spend immense amounts of money targeting their promotional advertising to specific subgroups in order to make an impact with a highly targeted message. Similarly, your dissertation has to focus on a research question that will be meaningful and doable. The following activity helps you along this process of moving your dissertation from a blob into a path.

## TRY THIS! DISAGGREGATE THIS!

This activity will help you to clarify and concentrate your dissertation idea. This activity is best done one-on-one with a peer who has some knowledge of your topic or the educational field in general. Follow this basic step-by-step format: the first person writes down—in one or two sentences—his dissertation idea and tells it to the second person. The second person asks a series of scripted questions, beginning with a basic opening format (see the suggestions in Column A) and ending with a basic closing dichotomy between two or three groups (see the suggestions in Column B). The first person attempts to answer each question (it's okay, of course, to answer "I don't know"). Upon completion, the partners switch roles and repeat the activity.

| Column A | Column B |
|---|---|
| Will this focus on . . . | Girls or boys? |
| Does this take into account . . . | Elementary, middle, or high schools? |
| Will this impact . . . | Certified or uncertified teachers? |
| Did you think about . . . | Urban, suburban, or rural schools? |
| Will this work for . . . | Large or small schools? |
| Does it matter whether . . . | First- or second-language learners? |
| | New or veteran teachers? |
| | Children from single-parent or two-parent families? |

The fundamental point of this activity is to force you to think about all of the multiple variables that may affect your dissertation. The key is for the second person to come up with as many potential differences in Column B as possible. This will help the first person to realize whether he has thought through all of the permutations and options available for analysis. This process is analogous, at a basic level, to a formal literature review, which allows you to research the variables that have indeed been found to impact and be relevant for your dissertation topic. For now, though, it is extremely helpful to begin such a process of disaggregation to help you understand the complexities and possibilities of moving from the "dissertation blob" to a clearly defined vision of your dissertation focus.

## YOUR FIRST SUCCESS AT FOCUSING

### CREATING A TITLE AND RESEARCH QUESTION

While focusing and narrowing your dissertation topic will take a lot of work and time, this should not prevent you from moving forward with creating working drafts of two important components: your dissertation title and your research question. Note that you are just at the very beginning of truly focusing your dissertation research; as shown in Chapter 4, developing your theoretical framework, conducting your literature review, and choosing your research design and methodology will be crucial to structuring and finalizing your research focus. We all have to start somewhere.

On a whimsical level, think of this stage as coming up with an off-the-cuff answer to the dreaded question that makes all doctoral students tongue-tied: "What's your dissertation about?" You want to go into a lecture about the historical context, explain the policy implications of your ideas, provide them with a stack of readings, critique a prominent line of thought, point them to how this relates to what was on the news last night, etc. They, though, just want one sentence. Maybe two. If they are interested, you could of course expand on your topic. But, really, being clear and concise about your complex project is a difficult skill to master. Nevertheless, this stage of tentatively formulating a dissertation title and research question is a wonderful place to begin to practice, for your sake as much as for those who innocently ask you such a question.

Coming up with such a phrasing should be viewed as a dialectical give-and-take of the formulation and reformulation of your dissertation focus. You should expect that the concise phrasing of your ideas will force you to rethink and revise your thinking. You will tell your title to others and have to answer their questions; you will look for research using your keywords only to find too little, too much, or not quite the materials you thought you would find. This back-and-forth—with your committee, other people, and the research literature—will make you realize that you need to revise specific keywords, alter the phrasing, or add a component that was seemingly tangential. This is a natural and normal process, and you should be prepared for the changes to come.

So, let's start with the dissertation title. A dissertation title acts as a synopsis of your research, synthesizing the key issues and/or findings. While you have not even begun your research, much less found out anything, you should by now have a set of focused keywords from your academic word bank and a fairly clear path for your research ideas. Your title should attempt to crystallize your stage of thinking at this moment in time in your dissertation progress. Moreover, it should actually contain the keywords for your review of the research literature, and these keywords, in turn, can perhaps even serve as the actual subheadings in the literature review section of your dissertation proposal. Think of each phrase in your dissertation title, as such, as individual seeds that will sprout into entire sections and ultimately comprise the second chapter of your dissertation.

Figure 3.4 provides examples of how two doctoral students used their dissertation titles as foundations for the questions that they wanted to address and analyze within the context of their own literature review. One doctoral student examined how elementary school teachers' special education referrals of African American boys may have been influenced by their attitudes about culturally relevant teaching. Another doctoral student examined the role of mentorship at an urban high school and the impact of such mentorship upon new teachers' career decisions to stay (or not) in education. In both cases, the students were able to use their dissertation titles as springboards for generating a whole set of questions that would then need to be answered through further research.

The generation of questions for further research is a wonderful entry into the academic literature. The keywords in the title serve as initial guideposts that are discussed in detail in Chapter 4. Likewise, you should now also formulate some initial research questions that will similarly

**Figure 3.4**    The Dissertation Title as Literature-Review Structure

Your literature review can and should be encapsulated within your dissertation title and subtitle and be based on the keywords in your academic word bank. I have outlined how two doctoral students began this process.

- *Example #1:* Race and Referrals: Teacher Attitudes, Culturally Relevant Teaching, and the Special Education Referrals of African American Males
  - **Teacher Attitudes:** What is the research around teacher attitudes to diversity and issues of race? How are such attitudes measured? What is the research on teacher attitudes to special education referral of students?
  - **Culturally Relevant Teaching:** What is culturally relevant teaching? What does the research say about its effectiveness? Is there any overlap with its relationship to referrals?
  - **Special Education Referrals:** What are the mechanisms for special education referral? How have they developed? What is the research about its use among diverse populations?
  - **African American Males:** What is the research specifically about African American males regarding academic success and special education?

- *Example #2:* Career Decisions: The Impact of Mentoring on Novice Teachers
  - **Career Decisions:** What does the research say about the decision-making process of teachers staying in education? What impacts such decisions? Do those decisions occur in different ways for different types of teachers at different stages in their careers?
  - **Mentoring:** What does the research say about the value of mentoring in supporting new teachers' career decisions? How is mentoring defined? What are the best practices, if any, of mentoring programs? How does mentoring fit into the larger research literature of induction?
  - **Novice Teachers:** What does the research say about novice teachers in general and their decisions to stay in education, specifically? What attributes of new teachers impact this decision? What attributes of the school environment impact new teachers' decisions?

guide your future choices of theoretical framework, research design, and research methods. The research question (or multiple questions) will ultimately become the key guide throughout your dissertation. Your dissertation research has to be able to answer the original research question posed and your advisor will work intensively with you to make sure that your final research question is phrased accurately and exactly and that the data you ultimately collect and write about do in fact answer your research question. Like everything else, we have to start by creating a tentative research question. A few key points will support this process.

The most important point, and one discussed at length in Chapters 4 and 5, is that your research question must be intertwined with your research purpose. The very basic question of "What do you want to accomplish with your dissertation research?" should not be answered in an open-ended, narrative way. In fact, there are actually only a few distinct ways that a traditional dissertation can approach and answer such a question. Specifically, there are four common and distinct ways to answer the question of research purpose—(1) exploration, (2) description, (3) evaluation, and (4) explanation. Each of these will imply a very different type and form of research question. For now, a brief summary of each will give a sense of how each one impacts the type of research question that can be initially developed.

An exploratory dissertation is interested in examining new or complex issues that have not yet been investigated in a particular way. This may be a new educational reform effort or the internal politicking between city hall and the superintendent's office. Research questions in an exploratory dissertation may thus be highly open-ended, allowing for multiple avenues of research to develop.

A descriptive dissertation focuses on clarifying and better understanding a particular educational issue, whether it is a curricular model, reform effort, or educational policy. A dissertation with descriptive goals asks specific "what" and "how" questions (e.g., "How has the whole-school reform effort impacted faculty and staff morale?") in order to focus the research methods and subsequent data collection.

An evaluative dissertation analyzes how well a particular program or practice is working. Such a dissertation may examine the particular needs that are (or are not) being met by this program or practice, compare such a program or practice to current "best practices" in the field, and analyze the gap between the current practices and the ideal best practices and available outcomes. The research questions for such an evaluative dissertation would be centered on the particularities of the specific program or practice under review, and focused on the key attributes and rubrics through which such an analysis is operationalized.

Finally, an explanatory dissertation has the goal of explaining why and how particular variables (e.g., teacher salaries, students' ethnicity, district-funding levels) relate to and influence each other. Evaluative-research questions are very tightly worded on the specific variables under investigation and the perceived relationship among such variables (e.g., "To what extent do teachers' years of experience predict normalized test-score gains in middle school pull-out science programs for at-risk youth?").

The specifics of each type of dissertation will be the focus in Chapters 4 and 5. For now, simply understand that your research goals will influence your research questions by the very essence of how a different type of dissertation purpose translates into a different type of terminology and research focus. To not attend to this is to risk creating a misalignment between your research question and your research goal. Your data may be fascinating, but they may have nothing or minimal to do with what you wanted to really study. As such, the more that you can be clear (for yourself and your advisor) about what you want to accomplish, the stronger and tighter will your dissertation become.

A second point to consider about your research question is that irrespective of the research goal, the question must be linked to the research and ultimately answerable. A research question should implicitly and/or explicitly reference the vast literature that probably already exists on your topic. Oftentimes, a research question accomplishes this simply by using the correct terminology in the correct context. If you focus on student dropouts, you should know the policy implications of and difference between using "event" and "cohort" dropout rates. If you focus on leadership styles, you should know the historical context and difference between "transactional" and "transformational" leadership.

Similarly, not using the correct terminology is also a sure sign that you are not yet familiar enough with the literature. If your research question discusses students' intelligence, to what exactly are you referring: to "g," which psychometricians talk about as general intelligence and differentiate between "fluid" and "crystallized" intelligence? To Howard Gardner's multiple intelligence? To Robert Sternberg's triarchic intelligence? To Daniel Goleman's emotional intelligence? To intelligence as a biological given or a sociocultural construct? It is critical to demonstrate a familiarity with the research by the way you phrase and the terminology you use within your research question.

Finally, there is a very specific maxim you should remember when formulating your research question: never create a question that can be answered in one word. In other words, don't phrase your research questions such that they can be answered with a simple yes or no. Put formally, your research questions need to be "robust" enough to allow nuanced answers to emerge.

The question, Does X intervention support students' academic outcomes? is poorly phrased because it only allows for a binary yes/no response; instead, the question can be phrased as follows: To what extent does X intervention support students' academic outcomes? Such modifiers (e.g., "to what extent," "in what way," "at what level") allow the researcher to gather and explore rich and complex data at multiple levels. Such flexibility, no matter how counterintuitive it may appear at the beginning, actually helps focus your work because it forces you to be clear about boundaries.

The seemingly problematic "openness" in a research question, by the way, is thus a false worry because it presumes the dissertation-as-blob view of dissertation research. As soon as you can clarify your parameters and your path through the "dissertation pyramid," this flexibility is actually an opportunity to explain exactly what path you will take and why you will take it. This is exactly how we know if we are ready to move forward.

# A FINAL THOUGHT

## FOCUSING YOUR RESEARCH AT A COCKTAIL PARTY

The next two chapters focus on clarifying your theoretical framework, conducting multiple literature reviews, and developing and choosing your particular research design and methodology. The key for now, though, is that you are able to focus and phrase your research as clearly and tightly as possible such that your research questions and purpose stand at the center of your thinking. You do not yet have to think through every permutation of your research or the literature or the variables involved. You just, for now, have to be focused enough in your research idea to be able to talk about it. This chapter thus concludes by describing an activity I conduct with my doctoral students. The "dissertation cocktail party" is a way to test the ability to articulate a research topic and move to the next stage in the process.

Here's the scenario and activity: you're at an elegant cocktail party and someone hands you a drink and says, "So, tell me about your dissertation. . . ." You should be able, on the spot, to clearly articulate your dissertation theme and focus. Your articulation should have nothing about methodology, theory, educational research, or any other so-called jargon. It should be about the big picture. Elegant people at fancy cocktail parties, I tell my students, don't really care about such minutia. If you can clearly and concisely answer this basic question, the inquirer then asks, "Fascinating . . . so what exactly will *you* be studying?" You should then be able to explain your research question in a few, clear sentences.

I go around the room and engage in exactly this kind of role play with each of my doctoral students about halfway through my Introduction to the Dissertation class. It takes a few attempts, but all of the students quickly understand how to reframe and rephrase their detailed ideas into such a conversational style. This is not just a fun classroom-based exercise; it is important to learn how to talk about your multifaceted and detailed ideas with others who may not be familiar with your research interests. Moreover, talking about it with others helps you clarify both the big-picture points and the exact terminology of why you are doing what you are doing. If you can't convince someone at a cocktail party about the value of your research project, you certainly aren't going to convince your dissertation committee.

My students get it. You can't just go deep into the literature and into the data and into your own writing. Your dissertation proposal has to be able to both go deeply into the specifics as well as "rise above the fray" in order to position the value and relevance of such work. They then ask the next logical question, "If indeed we were at a cocktail party talking about our dissertation, and the listener was truly interested, wouldn't another whole set of questions immediately arise? For example, wouldn't the listener ask us about whether this was ever done before or how we actually were going to do this study?" Yes, these are exactly the right questions . . . for the next chapter. Because, I explain, if the listener could ask such precise questions, then you have done an excellent job of precisely stating your dissertation idea. We can thus now move from focusing our research to actually structuring it.

# 4

## *Structuring Your Research*

**H**as this been done before? How are you going to do it? These are key and inevitable dissertation questions. You have great ideas, a strong understanding of the contextual issues surrounding your dissertation topic, and have begun to clearly formulate your main keywords. But how are you going to actually answer your research questions? Who else has done such research, in what contexts, with what populations, and with what relevance to your specific focus? How, moreover, are you going to conceptualize your own study, and how will this influence the data you collect and analyze? And, how will you link all of this together in a coherent and logical manner?

This chapter walks you through the steps necessary to begin to answer such questions in order to strengthen and synthesize your dissertation proposal. This involves, to put it formally, conceptualizing, researching, and operationalizing your study. This requires an initial understanding of diverse theoretical frameworks, the key components of a literature review, the distinctions across methodological perspectives (i.e., qualitative, quantitative, and mixed-methods design), and the overarching conceptual framework that will help you link together all of the key components of a dissertation proposal. The key point to remember throughout is that your research purpose impacts how you choose and work with each of these components. In turn, your choices will further focus and determine how you think, write, and talk about your research.

The first step in this process is thus to clarify your perspective, or "where you're coming from." For by now, you hopefully have a fairly focused topic or idea and likely believe that you can just jump straight into the literature review to see what's already been written on this issue. But hold on. What you also have to be able to articulate is not only what idea you are going to be examining, but from what perspective. This is your theoretical framework.

## CHOOSING A THEORETICAL FRAMEWORK

Even if you don't think you have, or need, a theoretical framework, you actually already do have one and use it all the time. To put it another way, believing that you don't have or need a theory is a theory in and of itself. To put it more formally, arguing that you don't have a theory is to believe that the world is an obvious and transparent place such that we can find the truth if we just search hard enough, with the right tools, and in the most objective and neutral way possible. Since the world just "is," you believe, there is really no need for a theory about it. This theory, by the way, is called positivism.

A quick way to show that the world is far from "obvious" is to look at how our society has changed its beliefs concerning a host of controversial issues, everything from whether women should be educated to gay marriage. For example, the answer to whether women should be educated was very obvious one hundred years ago: no, they shouldn't. For the next seventy or so years, though, the answer to this question was highly controversial. And for the last generation, the answer has again become obvious (at least in the Western world): yes, they should. To put it otherwise, the world is never an obvious place exactly because it is always seen through the eyes of individuals and their particular cultural and historical perspectives.

Educational research faces a similar situation. There is no "obvious" answer and response to any educational issue. Much depends on how we decide to look at a particular issue, at what level of analysis, and with what goals. Any particular way of looking at an educational issue is called a theoretical framework. Figure 4.1 provides an overview of the three main theoretical frameworks that are used in educational research. It should be noted that, just as with the descriptors in ERIC, each one of these theoretical frameworks has within it literally dozens of related theories and strands. Additionally, within each of these strands are dozens (if not hundreds) of scholars working to better define, articulate, and apply the specific theory to particular educational issues.

Your job as a practitioner scholar is not to become an expert in any of these three theories or their related strands. It is, instead, to realize which

**Figure 4.1**    Key Theoretical Perspectives in Educational Research

|  | (Post-)Positivism | Interpretivism | Critical Theory/"Posts" |
|---|---|---|---|
| **Assumptions About "Reality"** | An objective reality exists and can be correctly measured (with good enough tools) and adequately described (with clear enough language). | Reality is intersubjective in that it is socially constructed, such that it can be described and represented through diverse perspectives. | Reality is a function of dominant and implicit ideologies that determine how reality functions and potentially undermine the ideologies' own functioning. |
| **Assumptions About "Truth"** | Truth is objective. The key question is, What is the right answer? | Truth is constructed. The key question is, What is the meaning? | Truth is linked to power. The key question is, Who benefits? |
| **Key Goals** | Uncover the "right" variables that determine "best" outcomes. | Search for patterns of meaning. | Examine, expose, and/or overturn hidden relations of power. |
| **Key Outcome** | A number; a "best practice" | A story | An attack; an insight |
| **Unit of Analysis** | The variable | The act of meaning making | Categories of oppression (e.g., race, class, gender, sexuality); relations of truth making (e.g., knowledge, power, identity) |
| **Key Criteria** | Reliability, internal and external validity | Trustworthiness; authenticity | Theoretical consistency and insight; impetus for change |

one best fits your research topic and goals. In so doing, this will help you focus ever more on how to structure your research, where to look in the literature for solutions, and better understand the potential and limitations of your own topic. Just as importantly, clarifying your own theoretical framework is a crucial part of realizing one's own presumptions and blind spots about educational issues. All too often, our theoretical framework "chooses us" rather than the other way around, in that we take much about our world and our worldview for granted. Articulating a clear theoretical framework is thus immensely helpful because it exposes and unravels the assumptions and implications that go with "of course" seeing the world is a certain way. (See the Key Resources section on theoretical frameworks for key readings on these issues.)

Positivism is a perspective that developed in the mid-nineteenth century in response to, and as a standard bearer for, the era of industrialization and scientific thought. The word itself was coined by Auguste Comte, who founded modern sociology, in an attempt to describe the potential of "positively" guiding society through a scientific understanding of the social world. Positivism underpins our commonsense beliefs that the world and its workings can be known through objective, neutral, and rigorous means. It is a belief that we can truly figure out "what works" through the right procedures and practices, be it in the spheres of medicine, bridge building, or education. Positivism, to put it in the simplest of terms, is about finding the one best answer. Almost nobody, by the way, is an outright "positivist" anymore. Advances in the sciences have shown that we can never truly achieve 100 percent certainty about anything. Scientists now talk about probabilities (e.g., there is a "99 percent certainty") rather than "truth;" this has become known in the sciences and social sciences as "post-positivism."

Interpretivism may be thought of as a direct counterresponse to such a positivist perspective of the world. Arising to a large extent from cultural anthropology in the early twentieth century, an interpretivist perspective assumes that the world is not simply "out there" to be discovered, but an ongoing story told and refashioned by the particular individuals, groups, and cultures involved. A positivist researcher would simply go out and figure out the "truth"; an interpretivist researcher is, for better or worse, already part of the story about the truth because she is the one examining it and describing it. More forcefully, there is no single or authoritative "truth" from an interpretivist perspective since every group or culture privileges the truth of their particular viewpoint. An interpretivist perspective thus does not attempt to adjudicate between competing truth claims in order to determine the one best answer; rather, interpretivism suggests that all one can do is accurately and thoroughly document the perspective being investigated.

Critical theory—and responses to it such as postmodernism, poststructuralism, and postcolonialism (known as the "posts" perspectives)—is the most recent theoretical development and, as the name suggests, the most critical. Arising out of a group of thinkers known as the Frankfurt School in the years before and after World War II, critical theorists fundamentally question the neutrality and "good faith" of both the positivist and interpretivist perspectives. They suggest that, knowingly or not, such theoretical and research traditions perpetuate classist, racist, and sexist privileges. To argue that the world simply "is" or is a "story" erases the historical and contemporary reality that our current practices and policies were explicitly formed by (to put it bluntly) white, rich men. Thus, irrespective of such individuals' good will, their legacies and traditions inevitably contain the footprints and residue of a certain kind of privilege, which carries over into the success of individuals much like themselves.

The question for you is which theoretical perspective to choose and how to even begin to know by which criteria to make this choice. Let me, as such, provide you with two examples—the dropout problem and educational leadership styles—that may help to make vivid how any educational practice can be examined through these three distinctive theoretical frameworks.

The dropout problem in American schools has received enormous attention as scholars have recalculated statistics to discover that high-school graduation rates have not steadily risen in the last half-century as has been commonly thought (Fine, 1991; Greene, 2002). While experts continue to disagree over the exact figures, most by now agree that the best estimate is that 80 and 85 percent of all students graduate from high school within six years of starting ninth grade, though the percentages vary drastically across racial/ethnic groups: whereas for Asian Americans and whites the graduation rate ranges between 80 and 90 percent, for African Americans and Hispanics, it is between 50 and 60 percent. The stark discrepancy of these graduation rates across racial and ethnic groups is further exacerbated by the reality that high schools in many urban school districts see less than half of all students ever graduate; researchers have in fact found more than 3,000 of such schools, which they have dubbed "dropout factories" (Balfanz & Legters, 2004). There are many complex and intertwined educational, economic, and cultural reasons for why such dropout rates and disparities exist. What is crucial to realize is that, depending on your theoretical perspective, this issue can be approached in very different ways.

A positivist research perspective would attempt to focus on the primary variables that cause such dropouts and attempt to discover the best solution to lessening them. Research has shown, for example, that overage students are at much greater risk of dropping out of school. A dissertation project would then focus on figuring out the best form of intervention at a particular age group level. An interpretivist perspective, on the other hand, would focus on the deep details of how such overage students may feel awkward among their younger peers. An interpretivist dissertation may a yearlong qualitative case study that follows a group of overage youth to better understand the subtle mechanisms by which they stay in school or drop out. Finally, a critical theory perspective may examine how a particular group is disempowered in this process. Teenage girls who are pregnant, for example, seldom return to school and graduate upon the birth of their child. A critical theory dissertation may examine (or develop) interventions such as in-school child-care facilities that can support and empower the success of this all too often disenfranchised population.

Another example comes from data and research about leadership theory and leadership styles (e.g., Bolman & Deal, 1991; Senge, 1996). A major aspect of preparing today's educational leaders—principals, super- intendents, and other key administrative personnel—is honing their abil- ity to be "transformational" leaders who create change through data-driven decision making within highly complex and contested public and political terrain. Given the level of high-stakes accountability and standards-driven curriculum and instruction, educational leaders have very little margin of error in what they do, how they do it, and the timeframe within which they do it. There are, moreover, oftentimes multiple and conflicting goals that educational leaders must adroitly balance. For example, educational leaders must balance increasing student test scores against the threat of overly narrowing the curriculum or inhibiting student-centered instruc- tion; fostering stronger professional learning communities without over- burdening already-busy teachers and staff; supporting equitable distribution of resources for all students without being mired in local poli- tics, or community pressure, to privilege one student group over another.

A positivist research perspective may examine any one of these vari- ables to determine, for example, the most effective and efficient use of a principal's time or resources. A statewide survey of principals may shed light on the perception of the relative value of an hour spent on attending a parent association meeting, versus partaking in a professional develop- ment opportunity, versus catching up on e-mail correspondences. An interpretivist perspective may instead shed light on the perceived benefits and demands of today's fast-paced job. Given that the average tenure of an urban superintendent is less than four years, it is urgent to understand why so many individuals leave or, perhaps, the qualities of those that stay for a decade or more. Finally, a critical theory perspective may question the very framing of "transformational" educational leadership. Such a disser- tation may explore the latent male-centered notions of what constitutes "leadership"; this may be particularly relevant given that 90 percent of all elementary teachers are female, yet more than half of all elementary prin- cipals are male. Or it may question how such a top-down perspective undermines and mutes deliberative and democratic school cultures.

The point here is that irrespective of one's dissertation topic, there are multiple perspectives that are distinctive from, and oftentimes contradictory with, each other. And, to say it yet again, you can't try to cover all of them in your dissertation. You must instead carefully reflect on your goals for your dissertation and how you have phrased your research focus. Are you trying to solve a problem? Better understand a situation? Question the way things have been done? Each of these questions will necessitate different theoretical frameworks.

At some level, this choice is arbitrary. An excellent dissertation can be written about a specific intervention for overage dropouts, or a case study of a particular group of at-risk youth or the critical analysis of state-level educational policy for pregnant teens. The key is that the research question is focused, manageable, and not trivial. And, of course, that you are passionate about it. But arbitrary does not mean random, for almost all theory is what is known as "underdetermined." In other words, the same data can be fruitfully examined from more than one theoretical framework. (Almost all basic astronomy and navigation can be done just fine using two-thousand-year-old calculations from Ptolemy, who was assuming that the earth was in the middle of the heavens.) So long as the larger issues in the dissertation, the research question, the theoretical framework, and the methodology are all aligned, the decision about which theoretical framework to use rests on the specifics of your particular focus.

The key is that everything flows from what you deem to be the true "key outcome." What is goal of your dissertation? Is it to solve a problem (a post-positivist perspective)? To question a taken-for-granted program (a critical perspective)? The key outcome of your dissertation focuses everything else both by a means of exclusion (you can't do X if you want to figure out Y) as well as by focusing the parameters. To return to the dissertation-as-path analogy, choosing a theoretical framework will allow you to focus your academic word bank even more. You may not yet have a path through the levels of your pyramid, but the number of possible paths should drastically decrease. The next step is to see what other researchers have written about your topic from your particular theoretical framework. This is what is known as the literature review.

## DOING A LITERATURE REVIEW

The literature review is, simply put, your chance to make sure that you are not wasting your time. You may by now have articulated a fairly focused research question within a particular context and from a particular theoretical framework. But what if someone else has already researched and written about the exact same thing? Or, more likely, what if someone has analyzed this particular issue in a way that better sheds light on the specific issue you are intending to examine? There is no reason, for example, to look at seven different variables concerning the "best practices" of dropout prevention if a vast amount of research suggests that there are in fact just three key variables to focus on.

A literature review, moreover, may act as a rationale for your own research. You may find that lots of research has focused on the importance of full-service schools for immigrant populations, but nobody has actually ever done any research on what the immigrant community itself believes are important resources to have within a school building. Your dissertation would thus describe and analyze existing research and note that there is a very specific gap in the literature which, you hope, your dissertation research will address. Finally, a literature review serves as an inspiration (and caution) for your own research. By examining others' research, you can begin to see the way others have framed similar issues, the methodologies they used, the difficulties encountered, and the solutions found. This is an invaluable lesson as you begin to move forward with your research project.

It is important to realize that there is no *one* literature review. There are, in fact, multiple levels of literature reviews that may be thought of as a progressively focused downward spiral. Specifically, conducting a literature review is a multistage process that requires different foci at different points in the process. Figure 4.2 provides a framework for the stages of a literature review. This should be viewed as a heuristic, semistructured guide that can help you focus and structure your research question(s).

The key is to realize that different literature searches should be conducted at different points with different goals and outcomes. I differentiate the search for literature on two distinct spectrums: general versus academic searches and practitioner versus scholarly searches. A general search

**Figure 4.2    Conducting Multiple Literature Reviews**

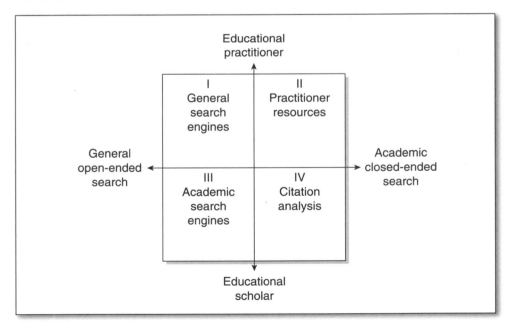

is an open-ended search, whether this is done through traditional search engines such as Google or through academic search engines such as WorldCat; an academic search, though, is closed-ended to the extent that it is done based on someone else's synthesis, whether this is an organization's resource list or a scholar's reference list. The spectrum between practitioner and scholar searches is then a simple differentiation between generally available resources (again, like Google or an organization's Web site, such as the Association for Supervision and Curriculum Development [ASCD]) and more scholarly resources such as academic search engines and specific peer-reviewed journal articles.

In general, I advise my doctoral students to go sequentially through each research stage with different goals and expectations to allow a natural progression in developing a research focus. To put it schematically, a general open-ended search should lead you to numerous practitioner resources that will have compiled and synthesized a host of key research on the main topics and themes you are exploring (thus moving from stage 1 to stage 2); this compilation, in turn, should point you directly to academic articles and keywords that you can then use as the basis for your open-ended academic search (thus moving from stage 2 to stage 3); this open-ended academic search, in turn, should reveal a wide variety of academic writings that you can carefully read and then use their reference lists to find additional key sources and directions (thus completing the literature-review process by moving from stage 3 to stage 4).

The first level of review should be conducted at the idea-formation stage to help you begin to understand the overview of the field. This can be done through simple Web-based search engines such as Yahoo or Google. The goal here is not to read the thousands (or even millions) of links that pop up; it is instead to begin to see and cross-reference the individuals, groups, and ideas that emerge. It is very similar to how you created the academic word bank in ERIC. In the literature-review stage, though, you should be compiling a list of practitioner resources—for example, organizations, Web sites, workshops, curricular materials—that appear to consistently come up whenever you do a general search with your key terms. If I as a principal am interested in developing a strong professional learning community in my elementary school, a general overview search may provide links to articles in *Education Week,* an ERIC Digest that summarizes this issue, or to the Web site of the National School Boards Association (NSBA), where they have a policy brief about this issue.

It thus becomes possible to move from an open-ended search into a closed-ended one. Accordingly, you should now review and research each of these "practitioner resources" that you compiled in the first round of review. You may peruse practitioner magazines and journals such as *Educational Leadership* and *Phi Delta Kappan* as well as surf around the Web sites of national umbrella organizations such as ASCD, NSBA, or the Council of Chief State School Officers (CCSSO). The goal is to become familiar with some specific subfields and key terms within your particular dissertation topic, as well as compile an initial list of key readings and research. Oftentimes, in fact, such magazines and organizations have an entire research section (often termed "research," "publications," or "resources") that can be extremely helpful. Compiling such resources is a completely legitimate and effective strategy; there is no need to do a massive and potentially fruitless search in academic databases when other researchers and organizations have done the work for you. This does not mean that you are now done with your research; you can't just cut and paste their resource list into your own reference list. Rather, what you have now done is compile a focused list of terms, authors, and key research that will guide the next stage of your literature search.

The next stage of a thorough literature review is to move into an open-ended search using traditional academic research tools and search engines such as ERIC and Google scholar, and library search engines such as JSTOR and EBSCO. I want to highlight that this should be the third stage of your literature review, and not your first. Doctoral students often make the common and highly problematic error of beginning at this stage in the literature review and, as such, they quickly become overwhelmed by the educational jargon, immense number of citations, and lack of clear direction. They do not realize that they first have to create the equivalent of an academic word bank of ideas in order to focus their topics and searches. If you have done the first two stages of the review, though, you should know exactly the academic terms and author names to enter in these academic search engines.

Doctoral students tend to get discouraged, moreover, because most academic articles and books are very narrowly focused, examining one very small issue in a very specific way. There are few big-picture pronouncements, little direction for how to apply or extend the findings, and minimal attention to writing for a general-practitioner audience. Put otherwise, academic articles and books are kind of like dissertations. The educational scholars you should by now be reading have done what you are about to do: they have focused and narrowed their research questions, chosen an appropriate theoretical framework and methodology, conducted a comprehensive literature review, and conducted a careful study on a highly delimited question. Research studies, for example, may be able to say a lot about a specific reading intervention in a third-grade classroom, but very little about the strengths and weaknesses of conducting reading intervention in general.

This is their biggest strength (and weakness). To return to the dissertation-as-path analogy, a good research study should be able to either cut one or two keywords or topics from your overarching dissertation focus or give you a more focused path to follow. If you have been thinking about researching the role of reading-intervention programs to support the success of at-risk elementary students, a particular research study may have focused on one-on-one versus group work as the intervention; another study may have investigated the intervention's applicability to Hispanic or African American youth; another study may have examined the implications of doing such an intervention in third- versus fourth-grade classrooms; and yet another study may have examined whether the gender of the teacher matters in such interventions. None of these studies give a "final" and definitive answer about whether the reading intervention "works."

Rather, each study has taken a very careful approach to examining a sliver of the entire pie. And each of these studies can then be used to support your own arguments about the need for your particular dissertation focus. Your goal in this third round is thus to find as many academic reports, articles, and books that examine your particular dissertation focus from as many (slightly different) perspectives as possible. One research study may have focused on a "best practice"; another may have been describing the perspectives of the students within that specific intervention; and yet another study may have been a theoretical critique of such an intervention. All of these are wonderful studies that you will need to read and incorporate into your literature review.

Finally, such a compilation of academic resources through the academic open-ended search will bring you to what I think of as the final stage of a literature review: the analysis of citations. Every research document you are using should have a bibliography or reference list that is used to support and substantiate its own claims and arguments. You can simply go through these lists in order to compile an additional list of authors you want to read and research, as well as determine which of these may be cited multiple times and are therefore probably key to focus on. This citation overlap is in fact very common, as numerous research studies in a particular subfield all point to a few classic authors or reports. This type of review, then, will help you to articulate key and recent developments, discover gaps in the field, and develop critiques and potential new directions for your specific topic.

---

**Hint! Differentiating Between a Reference List and a Bibliography**

It is important that you know the difference between a reference list and a bibliography. A reference list is a list of the works cited in your dissertation. If it's in the main body of your dissertation (what's known as an "in-text" citation), it should be listed in your reference list. Likewise, if you have something listed in your reference list, make sure that you have cited or quoted from it somewhere in the text. Alternatively, a bibliography is a list of all of the relevant texts that you have read about an issue but which may not be cited in your dissertation. A final dissertation should usually only have a reference list. A bibliography is much more common at the comprehensive-exam stage, where you want to show your faculty the breadth and depth of your reading in a specific subfield. It may also be used in a dissertation proposal for a similar rationale (though check your institutional guidelines to be sure).

## Hint! Knowing When Your Dissertation Idea Is Focused Enough

I remember reading a fascinating article about the criminal justice system in *The New York Times Magazine.* I kept nodding my head every time the author made an interesting point. "What a great and insightful article," I thought to myself. A week later, the magazine published several letters to the editor that were deeply critical of the author's arguments, assumptions, and conclusions. These writers (professors of criminal justice, according to their bylines) marshaled data and offered persuasive alternative arguments. "Good points," I thought to myself, "I hadn't thought about it that way." I was convinced. The following week the magazine published a response from the author to these letter writers. The author went step-by-step through the critiques and explained (very nicely, I thought) why he wrote what he did and why he could substantiate it. At this point, I gave up. I had no clue anymore as to who was right and who was wrong. Put otherwise, I realized that I had no expertise or grounding by which to begin to even figure out which side was more "right."

The point of this little anecdote is that if you are still nodding your head and agreeing with every article or book you read, then you are not yet focused enough to move forward. The whole point of analytically disentangling your dissertation idea into keywords, settling on a helpful theoretical framework, and doing a substantial literature review is so that you can begin to understand the multiple ways to think about your topic, and how different perspectives have different assumptions and implications. You should be able—unlike me with the criminal justice article—to articulate how a specific argument "plays out."

Specifically, this fourth level of review can help you begin to become familiar with the key authors and ideas in your specialization, as well develop a sense of what may be missing in the research. If, for example, most of the literature on a specific reading intervention is quantitative in nature (i.e., focused on the statistical analysis of whether or not it works), there may be a real need to offer a qualitative analysis that examines a case study of how such a reading intervention is implemented by a teacher or experienced by a particular group of students. Likewise, you may find that no one has yet examined a particular leadership initiative from a feminist perspective.

While it is not necessary to follow this exact order or use the exact search methods outlined here, it is crucial that, at some point in the dissertation process, you make sure to cover each of these areas. In doing an open-ended search in academic search engines (a third-level review), you may even find yourself intrigued by a seemingly tangential article. You may then go back to a first level review and do a general search on the idea to see where this may take you. Thus, much like a sine wave, you will continue to go deeply into a topic only to return to the surface to explore a new direction or idea. With each step, you should be slowly focusing your idea, weeding away interesting but ultimately tangential topics, and understanding how your own topic links to comparable and parallel topics and ideas.

Finally, regarding the literature review, there is no failsafe way to say when you should stop this process. And in some way, to be honest, your literature review should never really stop. You should always be searching out new research that may apply to your topic and make it more relevant or focused. Many of my students actually find that they cannot stop themselves once they get started; every educational news story or research study becomes an opportunity to think about their particular ideas from a new angles. The key is to examine the vast majority of research in your specific dissertation area, and understand the issues that surround it. This may be thirty or fifty, or even one hundred different studies. The key is that you can delineate what that specific topic is and who else has written about it.

## UNDERSTANDING RESEARCH METHODOLOGY

Your literature review should help focus the direction of your research. Your methodology will now help you to answer how you will actually accomplish it. While much about your methodology can (and should) be highly detail-oriented and technical, it can also be summarized as an answer to the simple phrase, "How will you actually do that?" Thus, before we delve into the specifics of research design and diverse methodological frameworks, it is helpful to begin to talk through, in a general and descriptive fashion, what exactly you envision yourself doing. At the heart of any research project is the key step of translating an idea into a specific procedure, question, or term. This is known as "operationalizing" something, or making it measureable. We may be interested in a host of key questions: whether a specific curricular intervention raises test scores, whether cross-racial interactions between teachers and parents in an urban school are detrimental to parental involvement in school, or to what extent revolving district leadership negatively impacts organizational culture. To begin to answer such questions, I ask my doctoral students to engage in the following activity.

This activity allows students to articulate their ideas in a narrative fashion and not be constrained by specific educational methods or protocols. Ideally, this "simple" articulation can actually serve as both the basis and conclusion for the methodological aspect of the dissertation; that is, once my doctoral students understand all of the intricacies, research designs, and options, they should be able to restate their narrative knowing full well that, if prompted, they could go deeper into any aspect to explain the details. You should be able to do this as well by the end of Chapter 5. For now, the narrative serves as a starting point. The next step is thus to go deeper into the actual research methods that are available.

## TRY THIS! CAN YOU OPERATIONALIZE THAT?

This activity will help you articulate the process of actually collecting your data. This activity is best done one-on-one with a peer who has some knowledge of your topic or the educational field in general. Follow this basic step-by-step format. The first person writes down his dissertation idea/title and the outcomes hopefully achieved by this dissertation (e.g., student achievement, parental involvement, understanding of the culture at the district office). For each specific outcome or issue raised, the second person then asks the question, "Can you operationalize that?" (i.e., "How will you get that specific data?"). The first person attempts to answer each question (it's okay, of course, to answer, "I don't know"). Upon completion, the partners switch roles and repeat the activity.

The following example may be helpful. One of my doctoral students wanted to examine how several alternative high schools in an urban school system were supporting at-risk youth. Her initial research question was, To what extent do the four alternative high-school settings in the [Urban School System] foster educational success and what structures and practices in these alternative high schools support those successes? I thus began to ask her to operationalize what she meant by "success." By using the district's own language, she came up with a host of practices that constituted success: effective instruction, shared leadership, family engagement, etc. I then asked her to operationalize each of these. What exactly does effective instruction look like? How would I measure it? By what criteria? Again, using the district's own language, she began to operationalize the characteristics of each of these practices. In so doing, we were able to create multiple means (e.g., school visits, teacher surveys) that would measure the characteristics of each of these practices. A draft of the initial data matrix is below.

### Matrix 1: Effective Instruction

| | Surveys | | | Interviews | | | | | | |
| | School Visits | Class Observ. | Teacher | Principal (in person) | Teachers (by phone) | Parents (by phone) | Students (focus groups) | Documents | Journal |
|---|---|---|---|---|---|---|---|---|---|
| 1. Culturally relevant instruction | Yes | Yes | Yes | Yes | Yes | Yes | Yes | Yes | Yes |
| 2. School climate | Yes | Yes | Yes | Yes | Yes | No | Yes | Yes | Yes |
| 3. Student engagement | Yes | Yes | Yes | Yes | Yes | No | Yes | Yes | Yes |
| 4. Professional learning community for adults | Yes | Yes | Yes | Yes | Yes | No | No | Yes | Yes |
| 5. Engaging learning environment for students | Yes | Yes | Yes | Yes | Yes | No | Yes | Yes | Yes |

## CHOOSING A RESEARCH METHOD

A research method is nothing more (or less) than a tool to help you answer your research question(s). The research question serves to constrain and contain what you will subsequently do, so you should be aware of the different modes and terminologies by which research is carried out. This overview, though, should not be used as the only basis for making decisions or carrying out your research, as there are a large number of resources that delve deeply into each aspect outlined below (see the methodology section in the Key Resources). The main distinctions to be aware of are those between empirical and theoretical research and, within empirical research, between qualitative and quantitative methodology (see Figure 4.3). It has also become quite common to use both methods either concurrently or in stages; this is known as mixed-methods research.

**Figure 4.3**  Overview of Research Methods

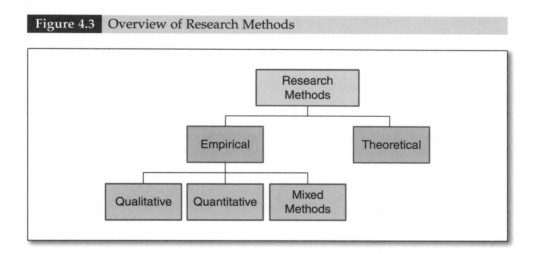

Most educational research is empirical; that is, it examines specific data, such as test-score results, teacher surveys, or parent interviews—and I will as such focus on empirical research methods. Nevertheless, it is important to understand the value of a theoretical dissertation. A theoretical dissertation also uses "data," though data here is understood as the specific body of literature that is examined, analyzed, critiqued, synthesized, etc. To put it visually, the doctoral student doing a theoretical dissertation finds his data in the library (or, more likely, online), while the student doing an empirical dissertation finds her data "in the field."

Let me provide two examples of theoretical dissertations. I am currently working with a doctoral student ("Michael") who is examining the potential relationship between zero-tolerance policies in schools and the expansion of the so-called school-to-prison pipeline over the last two decades. He is using multiple conceptual lenses (technical, critical theory, and critical race theory) to examine a host of literature on each of these distinct areas. He is not collecting data on youth dropouts or recidivism rates in a particular school, school district, or state; he is not interviewing teachers, parents, youth, or criminal justice experts; he is not conducting surveys of special education coordinators, local ministers, or parole officers. There is no empirical data. Rather, he is looking at two distinct bodies of literature—zero-tolerance policies and the school-to-prison pipeline—through three distinct, conceptual lenses. What is distinctive about his study is that it brings together two discussions that are very rarely talked about together; also, he is analyzing these discussions through three perspectives that provide highly divergent "answers" to the relationship between zero-tolerance policies and the juvenile justice system. Such divergence, in turn, reveals much about our seemingly commonsensical notion of the role of zero-tolerance policies in schools.

Another one of my students ("Carline") recently completed a dissertation that examined the "gaps" in holistic education. There has been, since the 1970s, a growing field of holistic education that is aligned to, and synergistic with, a wide range of current educational movements such as multiple intelligences, project-based learning, and differentiated instruction. Yet, no systematic research informs the holistic-education field about the most pressing issues to examine or what research areas are least developed. Carline's dissertation was thus a comprehensive search for, and examination of, the key literature in the field and a systematic mapping of where such literature was strong—such as in curriculum development—and where there were gaps—such as assessment practices.

These examples of theoretical dissertations, you may have noticed, do not seem as "urgent," applied, or school based. They appear more "abstract" and, perhaps, more like a traditional PhD dissertation. And in some sense they are, in that (as I mentioned at the beginning) there is no explicit and firm boundary between PhD and EdD research. Yet, it is crucial to note that these issues are deeply relevant and prominent for these doctoral students. Carline was the longtime principal of a small private school that prided itself on a holistic-education philosophy and practice. Yet, she had never really delved deep enough to truly understand what that meant or how it played out in the classroom, in working with parents, etc. This was her chance to do so in a meaningful way and contribute to the evolving literature in the field. Likewise, Michael, an African American school psychologist in an urban school system, has seen the implications of zero-tolerance policies and the expanding number of youth in the criminal justice system up close. His dissertation was a chance to work through the relationships between these two seemingly disparate developments.

Doctoral students may be disinclined to do a theoretical dissertation because it may not seem relevant enough or be "exact" enough. There appears to be no "right" answer. Yet, as I will explain below, no dissertation—be it theoretical or empirical, qualitative, or quantitative—is ever truly "true." All dissertations are attempts to delineate a specific worthwhile problem, be clear about the scope of the research, and provide a nuanced and careful examination of the issue—all to the satisfaction of other educational scholars knowledgeable about the issues (who, in this case, are on your dissertation committee). A theoretical dissertation can do this just as well as an empirical dissertation. It may be a little harder to accept that one does not "collect data," that one spends the vast majority of time reading and thinking, or that one cannot have a definitive answer at the conclusion of the process. But, it is just as legitimate, relevant, and potentially powerful. Well-done theoretical dissertations offer just as much, if not more, to educational research and practice as well-done empirical dissertations.

David Berliner (2002), for example, has argued that educational research suffers from what he terms a "findings by decade" problem. Much research done ten or twenty years ago, he points out, is often useless for current scholars and practitioners. In one respect, you might think, data are data are data. If a certain type of curriculum or intervention worked twenty years ago, why shouldn't it work today? The answer is that our conceptual lenses have changed. All data are theory bound. Researchers discovered in the 1960s that teacher expectations (what is oftentimes called the "Pygmalion effect") played an immense role in how they taught certain kids and, in turn, how well those children did in school (Rosenthal & Jacobson, 1968/2003; Goldenberg, 1992). Likewise, researchers in the 1980s discovered and documented just how male-centric much of our pedagogy really was, and how this negatively impacted girls' success in school (e.g., American Association of American Women [AAUW], 1992; Sadker & Sadker, 1995). Researchers (and teachers, principals, superintendents, and parents) could no longer do "business as usual." All of a sudden, how teachers behaved and the expectations they held for certain groups of children had new meaning. All of a sudden, all teaching styles had to be examined for whether boys and girls were being taught equally and equitably.

The "data" themselves did not change. Low-income children who came to school wearing secondhand clothing and speaking a slightly different way still underperformed compared to their richer peers. And girls continued (at least for several more decades) to underperform compared to boys across almost all academic subjects. But, the explanation for why this was occurring changed. The research that documented the Pygmalion effect and male-centric curriculum did not in and of itself transform educational practice. Instead, what each of these conceptual breakthroughs accomplished was to help provide a more nuanced and careful understanding of classroom dynamics and instructional practices. In doing so, such research changed how we view and talk about an immense amount of K–12 education. Such theoretical contributions are thus critical to educational research and certainly worthwhile to carry out.

## EMPIRICAL METHODOLOGIES

If you plan on conducting an empirical dissertation, then you will need to become familiar with the terminology of qualitative and quantitative research in order to delve deeply into one or both of them. The (overly) simple distinction between the two is that quantitative research is about numbers (the "what," "where," and "when" questions) and qualitative research is about words and stories (the "how" and "why" questions).

A more accurate and nuanced explanation of these differences begins with acknowledging that each methodology answers very different types of questions at very different levels of analysis. Let's assume—to take an initial noncontroversial example—that I, the principal of a middle school, want to know my students' perspective about the cafeteria. I could ask one or two students about it, but an immediate and obvious problem would arise in that these students' perspectives might not be representative of the whole student body. I could thus go around and ask each and every student his or her opinion. This would solve the sampling problem, but I would quickly realize that the variety of opinions ("great," "disgusting," "I really like the beef enchiladas but the vegetables are usually soggy") would be next to impossible to compare and thus draw conclusions from. I could then choose a range of themes such as décor of the room, friendliness of the staff, freshness of the food, variety of meals, etc. and develop a standardized scale (5 is the best; 1 is the worst) to measure each and every theme. I could subsequently put this all in a survey form, distribute it to every student, and then compile and analyze the results. I might find that 80 percent of the students give extremely high scores to the lunchroom staff, but not a single student scores the variety of the food above a 2. I could bring this information to the cafeteria staff, thank them for their hard work, and begin to figure out how to add more variety to the menus.

I have just conducted quantitative research. It might not have been thorough or rigorous, but I was able to answer some very important questions about students' perspectives on a wide range of topics and, in turn, positively inform the practices at my school. And, if I gathered enough relevant data on the surveys and knew enough about statistical methodologies, I could begin to discern patterns such as whether boys have different preferences than girls and if students who come into the cafeteria earlier in the day have different experiences than those who come in later.

Now, let's add a twist. Let's assume that one of the reasons I am interested in these data is because I knew beforehand that the cafeteria staff consistently talked about being disrespected by the students. Yet, here are data that are seemingly contradictory: students responded overwhelmingly favorably about the staff. Was my initial knowledge wrong? Are the surveys inaccurate? I could revise the surveys and sent them out again, but how would I phrase the questions: Do you respect the cafeteria staff? Do you believe you treat them fairly? The immediate problem is that the students almost surely would not tell me the truth, especially because I am the principal.

So, I would have had to go deeper into this issue. Perhaps I would sit in a corner of the cafeteria over the course of several weeks and watch how students act. Perhaps I would interview a few of the cafeteria staff and ask them detailed questions about their experiences and how they feel about being treated in that way. Perhaps I might also gather a group of students and throw out the question, "So, tell me about the cafeteria staff?" and let them talk for a while. Perhaps I would ask my teachers for help and have them assign an "investigative journalism" project such that students write up articles about the cafeteria. I could then compile all of this information and see what patterns, if any, turn up. I might find, for example, that students feel overly hurried to make their choices in the cafeteria line and that staff don't appreciate the students calling them by their first names. I could then take these data and schedule an assembly to talk about courtesy and respect for teachers and staff, as well as work with the cafeteria staff to develop a new serving format.

I have just conducted qualitative research. It might not have been detailed or nuanced enough, but again, I was able to answer some very important questions about students' and staff's perspectives that positively informed the practices at my school. If I had spent more time sitting and watching or talking with additional staff and teachers, I might have discerned even subtler themes about how such cafeteria dynamics shifted depending on which teachers were on duty at the time, and perhaps whether such dynamics were tinged by racial or gender undertones, since most of my teachers were white males and females in their twenties and thirties and the cafeteria staff were all older, African American women.

I could have modified this example in a myriad of ways: the issue could have been whole-school reform or a new reading initiative; the population could have been parents or central administrators; the outcomes could have been higher test scores or a new public-policy initiative; the underlying themes could have been about age or immigrant status. The point is that empirical research is about gathering measurable data that is analyzable in different ways, at different levels, and for different purposes. Students' perspectives on a survey are just as measurable as the observation of a school setting. It is just measureable through different criteria and with different analytical procedures. We may think that a survey is more "objective" because we are dealing with numbers, but long-term observations supported by interviews can be just as valid. The key is to understand the research purpose.

The last forty years has seen immense methodological debates in higher education about which research method is "better" (e.g., Howe, 1988, 1992; Lincoln & Guba, 1985; Schrag, 1992). Thankfully, such debates have subsided as qualitative data have gained acceptance and researchers have come to acknowledge that both methodologies have their specific purposes and that one is not inherently better than another. It is this specificity to purpose that truly matters. Quantitative research methods, by their very nature of discrete quantification (e.g., using Likert=type scales from 1 to 5), allow for data gathering that can be extremely broad and take into consideration the opinions and perspectives of thousands of individuals. Qualitative research methods, by their very nature of attention to nuance and detail, allow for data gathering that can be extremely deep and take into consideration opinions and perspectives that may not initially be visible or obvious.

In each case, both methodologies have their strengths and weaknesses. Conceptually, each methodology is interdependent with the other: that is, my seemingly quantitative decision to circle 2 on the survey about the variety of the food in the cafeteria is a highly qualitative decision; my gathering of seemingly qualitative feelings and opinions can be quantified into a discrete group of categories, and these can then be quantitatively analyzed with standard statistical methods. Ultimately, therefore, it is not helpful to debate about the validity of one methodology over another. What is helpful is to determine which methodology is more valid for your particular study.

This is why, as mentioned, mixed-method design has become popular in educational research (e.g., Brewer & Hunter, 1989; Ragin, 1987). Put simply, a mixed-methods design is the use of both types of research methods—qualitative and quantitative—to collect more varied data and strengthen the validity of the final conclusions. (I am skipping over the often large theoretical and methodological hurdles and headaches of attempting to combine or interweave two distinct and oftentimes conflictual methodologies; it is worthwhile to at least become familiar with these issues if you decide to go in this direction [e.g., Bryman, 1984; Harding, 1987].) It is in this respect a pragmatic methodology (Johnson & Onwuegbuzie, 2006; Maxcy, 2003): it allows you the flexibility and power to employ whichever research model is necessary to answer complex educational situations that may be unclear until you actually begin to investigate them carefully.

One of my doctoral students, for example, sent out a survey to hundreds of teachers that investigated the relationship between their preretirement status, their feelings of contribution to their school, and their overall perspective of school culture. Her survey findings helped her to develop more specific questions which she then used in interviews (by phone and face-to-face) with a select group of teachers. From these interviews, she discovered that these teachers' professional development was key and mediated how they perceived many of the issues in her study. She was, as such, able to craft a new survey to help gather additional data from the large group of teachers. This back-and-forth between broad and deep data collection allowed her to ultimately present a highly nuanced and believable study with strong conclusions supported by a wide range of data.

Figure 4.4 provides a conceptual matrix for thinking about mixed-methods design. You may put more emphasis on qualitative or quantitative

| Figure 4.4 | Mixed-Methods Research Design |

|  |  | Time-Order Decision | |
| --- | --- | --- | --- |
|  |  | Concurrent | Sequential |
| **Emphasis of Methodologies** | Methodologies have equal status. | QUAL + QUANT | QUAL → QUANT |
|  | One methodology has primary emphasis. | QUAL + quant OR QUANT + qual | QUAL→ quant → QUAL qual → QUANT OR QUANT → qual → QUANT quant → QUAL |
| QUAL = Qualitative research  QUANT = Quantitative research | | CAPITALIZED = Methodology has primary emphasis Lowercase = methodology has secondary emphasis | |

*Source:* Modified from Johnson & Onwuegbuzie, 2006.

methodology; or, you may decide to treat them equally and spend as much time on one as the other as you move forward in your research. Moreover, some studies gather data sequentially, with (such as my example above) quantitative data collection informing qualitative data collection which, in turn, informs additional collection of quantitative data; or data collection can be done concurrently, such that fieldwork and surveys and interviews occur in parallel.

Irrespective of which model you ultimately decide on, though, the key is to realize that your research questions and goals should drive the methodology you ultimately choose, rather than the other way around. Just like you chose your theoretical framework depending on whether you wanted to tell a story or develop a best practice, your choice of methodology should be informed by the key outcomes you hope to achieve. Put otherwise, what type of data—numbers or stories or both—will best answer your research questions?

# LINKING RESEARCH PURPOSE TO RESEARCH METHOD

At this point, the key is to realize that your research questions, research purpose, research methods, and type of data are all integrally connected. Once you are able to clarify exactly what your dissertation is actually going to do (i.e., your research purpose), everything else falls into place.

This is because while there are an almost limitless number of dissertation topics, there are in fact very few methodological frameworks for answering the research questions within a dissertation. Most importantly, each framework is itself bound by and to specific practices, boundaries, and types. In other words, once you can articulate your key anticipated outcomes and the framework within which you will conduct the dissertation, a host of implications about dissertation goals, research questions, theoretical framework, and methodological design all "fall out" and help you focus and conduct your research. Figure 4.5 provides a schematic overview of the linkages between all of these components.

**Figure 4.5**    Linkages Between Key Dissertation Components

| Key Outcomes | Theoretical Framework | Research Purpose | Research Design |
|---|---|---|---|
| "Best practice" | (Post-)Positivism | Evaluation/Review | Quantitative |
|  |  | Explanation | Mixed methods |
| A story | Interpretivism | Exploration | Qualitative |
|  |  | Description | Mixed methods |
|  |  | (Evaluation/Review) |  |
| An attack | Critical theory | Exploration | Qualitative |
| An insight | "Posts" | Description | Mixed methods |
|  |  | (Evaluation/Review) |  |

The key here is that different perspectives and frameworks have greater affinity to and linkage with other methods and perspectives. Thus, for example, specific theoretical frameworks have more affinity to one form of research purpose rather than another. A post-positivist framework is much better suited for explanatory and decision-making goals than for exploratory analyses, which, in turn, are better accomplished through primarily quantitative or mixed-methods research. Alternatively, a dissertation that takes a critical perspective about a particular educational reform effort is better suited for using a critical theory orientation that aligns itself much easier to a descriptive research design carried out through qualitative means, rather than to a "best practice" quantitative analysis. To put the matter in even starker terms, a critical theory perspective usually attempts to undermine "best practice" formulations exactly because such so-called best practices are usually complicit with power structures that critical orientations are attempting to overturn.

These are not hard-and-fast rules. It is completely possible to use quantitative methodologies to support a descriptive research purpose with the goal of telling a story about, for example, the benefits of a particular elementary math curriculum. It is just that different goals are more effectively and efficiently accomplished in certain ways. This does not suggest that you do cannot "go against the grain" in your dissertation. I am simply helping you to see which way the grain goes. Moreover, as I discuss in detail in below, these linkages go in both directions. If I know that I want to conduct an exploratory analysis of district-level policy change, I can work backward to decide whether I am better able to tell a story about it or probe critically into such policy processes.

The research purpose, as discussed in Chapter 3, is intertwined with the goals of your dissertation and thus the research questions. And, the research questions, as noted, drive your dissertation. Everything from the literature review to the theoretical framework to the data collection and analysis should be focused on answering these research questions. That is the goal of your dissertation. It is therefore crucial that everything "lines up" in your dissertation; that is, there are logical and seemingly natural connections between each aspect of the dissertation design. Figure 4.6 provides a matrix of these relationships and interconnections. The matrix can be read from left-to-right if you are already clear on your research purpose, or you can begin with the framework you are already working within (your "guiding framework") and move outward to understand the implications for your research questions, research purpose, and methodology.

Before turning to the four specific research purposes, let us go through each category. The research purpose is the goal of the research study: Is it to describe an intervention or evaluate it? Is it to decide which intervention will impact the most students or is it to see whether the intervention works best with certified teachers? A dissertation may focus on any one of these four main research goals—exploratory, descriptive, evaluative, or

**Figure 4.6** Linking Research Purpose to Methodology

| Research Purpose | Research Question | Guiding Framework | Methodology |
|---|---|---|---|
| Exploration | Any combination of what, why, or how | Tentative hypothesis or emergent design | Primarily qualitative |
| Description | What or how | Categories | Mixed methods |
| Evaluation | How well is it working? | Needs analysis and/or gap analysis | Mixed methods |
| Explanation | Why? | Formal hypothesis | Primarily quantitative |

*Sources:* Based on and a modification of Shields (1998) and Shields and Tajalli (2006).

explanatory—and each of these goals should be understood as discrete and completely legitimate on their own. The research question is bound up with the research purpose. Exploratory research can ask a multitude of questions about the issues under study, whereas a descriptive study is by its nature phenomenological: that is, it is interested in the "what" question that allows full and complete description. The research question thus flows out of and uses the language inherent to the specific research purpose you are working with.

The research purpose and question are both informed and influenced by the guiding framework. The guiding framework can be understood as the conceptual underpinning of the methodology, just like the way you see the world (or your dissertation) is underpinned by your theoretical framework of post-positivism or critical theory (or whatever). If you want to explain or predict something (e.g., Does additional funding for afterschool programs increase in-school attendance for participating youth?), you are being guided by the notion of how a formal hypothesis works. If your goal is to evaluate and review an afterschool program, your guiding framework is based on how such a program does or does not align to the best practices for afterschool programming (technically termed a "gap analysis" in program evaluation). Finally, the guiding framework informs and constrains the type of methodologies that can be employed to gather and analyze data. It is now possible to detail each research type (i.e., your research purpose) and show how each type of research helps to focus on—and is interlinked to—the research question, guiding framework, and particular methodology.

An exploratory dissertation design is best used when an issue is not well understood in the literature or previously unexamined in a particular fashion. An exploratory design is best suited to qualitative research methods that allow for in-depth analysis of complex and layered issues and flexible enough to account for highly open-ended research questions, data collection protocols, and analyses. The guiding framework of a tentative hypothesis typifies the exploratory nature of the enterprise, in that certain hypotheses can be posed and reconfigured as data emerge or the situation is clarified. This is sometimes also known as an emergent design, whereby the researcher modifies the research focus and specific methodologies take into account new and unfolding information and findings.

Exploratory dissertations can be focused on the new: for example, the impact of the introduction of a new technology on classroom learning or the implications of a female leader in a historically male-dominated district. Exploratory research is also extremely useful for uncertain or controversial issues: for example, community perceptions of English-only policies; teacher perceptions of the relationship between English language learners and special-education needs. Topics that do not have clear and definable boundaries or, alternatively, are so complex that any arbitrary boundaries will not allow a clear picture to emerge are prime examples of exploratory research's value and are one of the main reasons that these topics are difficult to conceptualize and implement (Becker, 1998; Collins, 1988).

Descriptive research is characterized by the deliberate and systematic articulation and analysis of issues presently lacking such clarity. Descriptive research is primarily concerned with explaining a phenomenon clearly through the construction of categories and order that can, in turn, support later action: for example, What has been the impact of a state takeover of a local school district? Once the impact can be determined—perhaps by distinguishing between impact on students, teachers, administrators, and the community—educators and policymakers may have a much stronger foundation for future actions. Descriptive research is guided by such categorization and ordering exactly because of the need to clarify complex data, and, as such, any and all methodologies that support such a goal are available for use.

An evaluative dissertation focuses on linking a descriptive design to a set of defined attributes and evaluating the correspondence. A common way to do so is through a program design model (e.g., Burawoy, 1998; Green, Caracelli, & Graham, 1989) that conducts a needs analysis followed by a gap analysis that analyzes the difference between (i.e., the "gap") the ideal "best practices" and the current practices of the program being investigated. This review format can be used across a wide range of situations—evaluating principals' leadership based on certain criteria, or reviewing whether reform efforts met predetermined conditions—by first defining commonly acceptable standards and then gathering and analyzing a wide range of data across each of these standards.

Finally, explanatory research focuses on finding a clear answer for why something occurs or how specific variables are related to each other: for example, Does leadership style impact teacher absenteeism? Does the gender of the teacher correlate with girls' perspective of science in middle school? Each of these formulations is grounded in a formal hypothesis that presumes and expects a research design that can account for and control extraneous and intervening variables as well as confirm the statistical significance of the connection. This is a signature practice of the social sciences in its ability (and presumption) to measure the impact of a particular intervention and thus influence practice and policy (Martin & Sell, 1979).

The value of clarifying these different research purposes is twofold. The first is the internal cohesion of each framework. In other words, once you are clear on what you want to do for your dissertation, you can simply and easily see the ramifications for the phrasing of your research questions, the type of methodology you are to use, and guiding framework that—whether you were first aware of it or not—underpins the methodology you employ.

The second value of this matrix is to realize that even the research purpose is itself influenced by the overarching theoretical framework and key outcomes you have for your dissertation. It thus becomes possible to link and draw out a host of nested relationships and connections between goals, research questions, and methodologies. Moreover, these relationships should not be viewed as if they were unidirectional (i.e., as if everyone should move from their theoretical framework to then determining the most apt research purpose and design). It is just as legitimate to do this process in the other direction. If you know that your goal is to evaluate the impact of a particular intervention—such as workshops to enhance the professional learning communities of your middle school teachers—then it is clear that you want to examine the best practice research of workshops in general and specifically the construction of professional learning communities. This is a post-positivistic theoretical framework in that you are looking to tinker with specific variables, such as the duration and depth of such professional development workshops, in order to have the most "bang for your buck."

Alternatively, if your current professional learning communities at the middle school level are mired in antagonistic relationships and petty squabbling, you may want to do an exploratory study to figure out why this may be occurring. If you are new to the school or simply want to have as wide a lens as possible to understand this problem, you may want to come at this issue from an interpretive perspective. If, though, you suspect it is due to past issues of racial unease or highly skewed power relations between male and female teachers, you may want to use a critical perspective (be it critical theory or feminist theory) to better understand and tease out the intricacies.

Structuring your research should now be close to complete. You should be able to articulate how you anticipate doing your study by distinguishing between a theoretical and empirical focus. If, as with most education dissertations, you will be doing an empirical dissertation, you can determine your primary research design and align a host of critical components in your dissertation proposal: research questions, research purpose, theoretical framework, methodology, and the guiding framework for your methodological design. These components form the heart of the dissertation proposal and serve as the scaffolding to build the specific research tools of your methodology. This is, in fact, the next step, as we move the discussion from the structure of the research to the actual tools you will use to collect your research data.

# 5

## *Conducting Your Research*

O ne of the main points in Chapter 4 was that one's research purpose is tightly intertwined with and linked by the theoretical framework and research design. This chapter takes the next step by showing the linkage between the research design and particular research tools. Specifically, to help you focus and choose among different tools, the key aspects of particular data collection methods and techniques are detailed. Moreover, also covered are the implications of such choices on the IRB process and how you should best prepare for meeting the needs of demonstrating that your research "does no harm."

## LINKING RESEARCH METHODS TO RESEARCH TOOLS

The data you collect will drastically differ depending on the research tools you use. Viewing an educational issue from a post-positivist perspective is fundamentally different from viewing it from a critical feminist perspective—likewise with data collection. If, for example, your goal is to analyze whether white teachers' racial attitudes negatively impact their interaction with nonwhite children, you will gain little by directly asking about their racial intolerance in a survey or even in an interview. "Excuse me, but are you racist?" doesn't really work as an interview question. Yet, there are some excellent indirect research techniques—measuring what is termed as implicit social cognition—that can indeed be used to gather valid data on individuals' race and ethnicity perceptions. Different research tools are thus valid for different research purposes, depending on your specific focus and topic. Figure 5.1 provides an overview of the four research purposes and how they are linked to different data collections methods.

Some data collection strategies (such as surveys) can be used across most types of research. Other methods (such as field observations), though, are really only applicable to a few types such as a tentative hypothesis or investigating whether a particular program aligns with best practices. Moreover, specific research purposes have fairly typical models for gathering data; thus the development of a formal hypothesis (X leads to Y) is most typically studied through a quasi-experimental design that makes use of data from existing statistical data as well as from surveys. While interviews and document analysis may be somewhat helpful if the hypothesis entails a very specific type of data, they are less common means of data collection; conducting field observations to "prove" that one variable impacted another is almost impossible and thus not done.

This overview can serve as type of decision tree whereby each successive decision—from theoretical framework to research purpose to research methodology to the specifics of each research tool—focuses and highlights the boundaries and direction for your particular study. While I cannot help you apply any of these particular tools to your specific situation or data, neither really can anyone else outside of your advisor and committee.

**Figure 5.1**    From Research Purpose to Research Tools

| Guiding Frameworks | Types of Research Tools | | | | | |
|---|---|---|---|---|---|---|
| | Quasi-Experimental (pre-/post-design) | Analysis of Existing Statistical Data | Surveys | Interviews | Document Analysis | Field Observations |
| Tentative Hypothesis | | (X) | X | X | X | X |
| Categories | | (X) | X | X | X | (X) |
| Needs Analysis | | X | X | X | X | X |
| Formal Hypothesis | X | X | X | (X) | (X) | |

*Note:* Marks in parentheses "(X)" designate a possible though not as common use of research tools for the specific research purpose.

Instead, the rest of this chapter offers guidance to understand what you need help with and what you don't when it comes to research tools and data collection.

## Quasi-Experimental Research

A quasi-experimental research design is a very common model in the social sciences, allowing the researcher to answer critical questions about the relationship between variables ("Did X cause Y?") and whether there are significant differences between variables ("Does group A perform better than group B?"). Also, due to the use of complex and seemingly accurate statistical procedures resulting in "statistically significant" conclusions (Cook & Campbell, 1979), quasi-experimental research is viewed as an appealing model because it provides seemingly concrete and "significant" results. (The terminology of a "quasi-experimental design" is used here because a true "experimental design" requires that the two groups being analyzed—for example, boys and girls—are randomly distributed. This is possible in medical research, where, for instance, one group of individuals receives the actual treatment, the other group receives a placebo, and neither group knows which treatment they are really receiving. This is not possible, though, in educational research as it would be logistically and financially difficult and ethically suspect.)

Quasi-experimental research designs can be extremely powerful if set up in the correct way. Specifically, quasi-experimental designs are usually used in one of three distinct ways: (1) they can describe the relationship between variables (such as whether there is an association between teachers' years of experience, having graduate degrees, and receiving higher performance evaluations); (2) they can determine whether a particular intervention (such as workshops for parents to support first-grade readiness) is successful; (3) they can explain whether a specific variable (such as teachers' years of experience) is actually predictive of another variable (such as receiving higher performance evaluations). Figure 5.2 provides a synopsis of these three different goals of a quasi-experimental design and the types of statistical procedures necessary to answer such questions.

There are four major points to understand a quasi-experimental research design: (1) the critical need for the disaggregation of data, (2) the distinction between correlation and causation, (3) the ability to "control for" variables, and (4) the term "statistical significance." Even if you are not going to use this type of research design for your dissertation, it will help to skim these four points. A highly ranked state-level administrator walked out of my course once, infuriated because she had just learned (after I lectured about this) that, over the years, she had wasted hundreds of thousands of dollars on consultants who never provided her with key information such as whether their findings had controlled for key variables or were statistically significant. Understanding

**Figure 5.2**    Goals and Procedures of Quasi-Experimental Designs

**Different Goals of Quasi-Experimental Designs and Relevant Statistical Procedures**

Description of Association ⟶ Correlation

Value of Intervention ⟶ Chi-squared; *t*-test

Explanation and Prediction ⟶ Regression

- **Correlation:** A correlation (there are actually two different types: *Pearson R* and *Spearman Rho*) tells the magnitude, direction, and statistical significance of the association between two variables. *Example*: Is there a relationship between the level and type of parental support and students' self-esteem?

- **Linear Regression:** This test determines which independent variables are significant (by "controlling for" each variable) in influencing the dependent variable and the level of that influence (known as accounting for the amount of variance). *Examples*: Does administrators' leadership style impact teachers' morale? Do the level, type, and duration of ambient noise impact students' test-score performance?

- **Chi-Square Test of Independence:** This test examines the association between two nominal variables, particularly whether such an association is statistically significant. (A nominal variable has no intrinsic ranking; e.g., gender, zip code.) *Examples*: Do middle school boys and girls have different expectations of body image? Do different ethnic groups vote differently for presidential candidates?

- **Independent Samples *t*-Test:** This test examines whether the means (i.e., average scores) of two independent groups (e.g., boys and girls) are statistically different from each other on any standardized measure such as a test. *Examples*: Do boys and girls score differently (on a nonrandom level) on the end-of-year state exam? Do whites and African Americans in community colleges score differently (on a nonrandom level) on the SAT?

these key distinctions impacts decision making at every unit of analysis, from the classroom to an entire state.

The disaggregation of data—much like the disaggregation of your dissertation idea discussed in Chapter 4—is crucial to the success of a quasi-experimental research design because you want to distinguish between huge numbers of variables (seen and unseen) to better understand why something is happening. One of my doctoral students, previously mentioned in another example, is examining whether teachers in the "preretirement" stage of their career (two to four years prior to retirement) still feel connected to their schools and are able to "give back" their many years of experience and knowledge. To examine this, she has to factor in how the age and experience of the teacher relates to other variables, such as the type of school they are in, the subjects they teach, etc., since the research literature has shown such variables to be influential. If she doesn't take such variables into account, her ultimate arguments would be less valid because she could not differentiate between different groups of teachers and their contextual situations. Her research may not "prove," for example, that teachers in urban schools are less able to "give back." Yet, not including such a variable would confound her findings to the extent that they become meaningless.

This gets at the second big issue and the one all too often confused both by the general public and even experienced researchers—namely, correlation is not causation. Just because two variables are related (such as years of experience in a school and the level of connectedness) does not mean that one causes the other. There may be a host of intervening variables (technically called "mediating variables") that impact the actual variables studied. Ice cream sales and sunstroke are probably strongly correlated, but this does not mean that you should avoid eating ice cream in order to avoid sunstroke. Both variables are instead simply correlated to summertime, so the season is the mediating variable in this example. In education, lower socioeconomic status is strongly correlated to lower success rates in school. But, convincing research (e.g., Berliner, 2006; Education Trust, 2006) demonstrates that a succession of good teachers and well-financed schools are mediating variables that can support success for youth from any socioeconomic level.

The ability to examine and account for mediating variables is technically termed as the ability to control for independent variables. (The dependent variable is the outcome variable; independent variables are all of the other things that can impact this outcome variable. See the corresponding activity on understanding this distinction and the implications thereof.) If you think that teachers' certification is what truly impacts students' test scores, you need to be able to account for (i.e., control for) lots and lots of other potentially intervening variables such as teachers' years of experience, their undergraduates grades, race, gender, etc. In other words, if you had two teachers of the same race, age, gender, etc.—with the only difference being whether or not they were certified—you could see if (after hundreds and thousands of examples) there were indeed differences across students' test scores. Several statistical procedures (such as regression analysis) can basically hold all of these variables equal except for one, by checking each variable on the list, and subsequently showing that a specific variable is indeed the one causing the impact.

## TRY THIS! UNDERSTAND DEPENDENT AND INDEPENDENT VARIABLES

The dependent variable is your outcome variable; independent variables are all of the other things that can impact this outcome variable. I use the following activity to help my students understand this important distinction: Draw two empty boxes on the board and label the right-hand box with the goal of "graduation" and ask for suggestions for filling in the left-hand box with variables that may impact the goal of graduating. Below is an example from one of my classes.

Finances
Support from advisor
Enough sleep
Getting good data
Etc.

GOAL
Graduating with my doctorate

My students provide examples ranging from the deeply serious ("having an important topic") to the comically hilarious ("remembering to eat"). Once several examples are provided, I clarify that the right-hand box is the dependent variable and on the left-hand side are some independent variables. I can also extend the exercise by helping them think about mediating variables: for example, you first have to be able to access a site before you can get good data. The seemingly linear relationship can then turn into a network of variables interacting with and linked to each other in complex and important-to-understand relationships.

Finally, implicit in each of the above examples is that every time two variables were stated as correlated or causally connected, what it really meant was that there was a "statistically significant" relationship between these variables. Scientists have realized that there is no way to prove anything 100 percent (discussed as part of post-positivism). Rather, researchers use the nomenclature that a relationship has to be nonrandom to a high degree of certainty; that is, if you do the experiment again and again and again, you will come up with more or less the same answer. Thus, when a relationship is "statistically significant at the .01 level," it means that we can be 99 percent certain that there is a real relationship between the variables rather than a chance occurrence. Note, though, that this does not yet mean that the statistically significant relationship is a large one or a truly meaningful one. That takes other research and analysis. But, at least it offers a first and important step in determining that the variables are indeed related.

These four points are immensely powerful for better analyzing and making use of data and for data-driven decision making. It is very common, for example, for newspapers and educators to cite test-score differences between two groups (e.g., boys and girls; whites and African Americans; certified and noncertified teachers) in order to prove a point or drive policy decisions. Yet, the differences across these groups are meaningless unless we know several other key points: Did the study take into account potential intervening variables, such as age, race, or level of school funding? Did the study find that the test-score differences between groups were as statistically significant? Was the study clear that results were correlational? Without this information, the findings are literally useless.

## Analysis of Existing Statistical Data

Quasi-experimental research is oftentimes done in real-time; for example, a teacher or principal sets up an intervention, such as teacher professional development or a new curricular design, and figures out whether it makes an impact (usually done through some kind of pre-/ post-methodology). It is just as possible, though, to do similar research with already existing data. Namely, schools and school districts often-times keep an immense amount of data over many years. This may be done due to federal requirements, because of state-level decision making, or simply as a by-product of a particular superintendent's initiative. Moreover, such data can vary immensely regarding its quality, comprehensiveness, and scope.

I was on a committee where a doctoral student used surveys to gather data on teachers' understanding and beliefs about culturally relevant pedagogy. She compared these findings with existing district data on the number, type, and frequency of special-education referrals made by these teachers. She was thus able to use several types of statistical tests to probe and analyze relationships between teacher characteristics (e.g., gender, grade level) and referral levels, as well as identify group differences. The access to district data offered a unique opportunity to examine a critical area, otherwise almost impossible to reveal.

This example suggests three key lessons when working with existing data. First, it is critical that the existing data be the actual raw data and not the summary or aggregate data. It would have been useless for this doctoral student to simply have the district tell her that, for example, there were twenty-seven referrals, made by twelve teachers in three years, across six schools. This summary would not have allowed her to link this information to the answers provided by individual teachers on the surveys. She instead needed to know which teachers made which type of referrals, at which schools, and in which years. In other words, she needed to see each data point about the referrals so that she could link it in her survey data set, which was disaggregated by teacher. Make sure, as such, that the data you want are specific enough.

The second point is a direct outcome of this need for such specific data. Namely, there are major issues surrounding access to data and the need for confidentiality and anonymity. The doctoral student only knew about and had access to these data because she worked in the school district and knew about these archived data and their level of specificity. Moreover, she had to ensure that she would not use any of the names of the teachers, students, or other individuals. She also had to make sure that no individuals were identifiable in the results. If you are using existing data sets, be cognizant that you will need to "scrub" the data clean of names and identifiable characteristics that may not be relevant to your particular study.

Finally, in compiling these data, you are basically creating a huge spreadsheet that becomes a complex yet analyzable data set. Your goal is to compile and add on as much relevant data as possible through as many sources as necessary and possible (the survey section below is an excellent means to do this). This is what I call "seeing the world through matrix-colored glasses."

Most post-positivist educational research is focused on explanations and predictions, so it needs to isolate one or more independent variables that are linked to a dependent variable. Such correlation or causational analysis (e.g., "What factors support girls' success in middle school science?") thus needs to adequately account for alternative explanations (i.e., mediating variables). Does, for example, the gender of the teacher matter? Does the girl's past performance in science matter? The only way to answer such questions is to make sure that as many relevant variables as possible are accounted for in your data set and can thus be tested. This is the key point: if you don't quantify it, it can't be in your data set. And if it can't be in your data set, you can't determine whether it was meaningful. As such, everything becomes viewed through "matrix-colored" glasses (see, e.g., Fraenkel & Wallen, 2003). This means that everything potentially becomes a variable that can be coded to become key data that can be gathered to fill in the gaps and add to the columns in this spreadsheet. Anything and everything becomes quantifiable in binary "yes/no" fashion or on some sort of scale. Figure 5.3 provides a simple template to visualize this mode of data collection and examination.

If your research concerns student academic outcomes, then each and every column in your matrix is an independent variable. Some of these variables may already be in existing data sets, whereas others can be easily gathered through existing surveys. Additionally, if students can be coded by some unique key (most school districts code students with a unique and random number that exists across all internal data sets), then it is possible to link multiple data sets and surveys such that you can combine academic variables (attendance, grades, etc.) with, for example, answers to opinion surveys.

One final ancillary benefit to viewing the world this way and entering such data into a data set is that you can very easily and quickly modify

**Figure 5.3**  Seeing the World Through "Matrix-Colored" Glasses

| | From Survey or Existing Data | | | From Survey | | | From Existing or New Data | |
|---|---|---|---|---|---|---|---|---|
| | **Demographic variables** | | | **Beliefs about** | | | **Scores on** | |
| | Age | Gender | Race | Body Image | Friends | School | Pre-test | Post-test |
| Student 1 | | | | | | | | |
| Student 2 | | | | | | | | |
| Student 3 | | | | | | | | |
| Etc. | | | | | | | | |

your analysis. Nothing prevents you, for example, from changing your dependent variable from students' posttest scores to their perspective on body image. This switch should certainly not be random, and it should be grounded in your particular research questions. But, if your data analysis reveals some unexpected findings and correlations across variables, it is very easy to redo statistical analysis to focus on other variables in other ways. Such flexibility and power is extremely beneficial to a comprehensive study.

## Surveys

Survey research is a very common tool in the social sciences for gathering data. Surveys appear easy to create, distribute, collect, and analyze. In many cases, they are. Especially with the rise of Web-based surveys (such as SurveyMonkey.com), distributing, collecting, and analyzing data from hundreds if not thousands of respondents is oftentimes as simple as clicking a button. Further, if you are using a premade survey that has already been validated and used in other studies, it may be extremely easy to make minor modifications and appropriate it for your own research study.

The problem here, though, as with every other research tool, is that research questions should drive research methods and tools, and not the other way around. Creating a good survey is actually an art form, just like every other research tool (e.g., Czaja & Blair, 1996). Despite surveys being ubiquitous in our lives and thus appearing simple to make and use, an immense amount of research (e.g., Berk, 1983; Howard & Dailey, 1979; Schwarz, 1999) has demonstrated that they are notoriously susceptible to error. Seemingly mundane and minor issues (e.g., 4-point rather than

5-point scales; the order of questions; whether done in person, online, on paper, or by phone) can all significantly affect how respondents may answer the exact same survey question. What thus appears simple and matter-of-fact is hardly the case. There are numerous books and Web sites that provide excellent guidance for survey design; thus, just two key principles can be kept in mind: carefully align your research questions, research literature, and survey questions and be sure to disaggregate your data based on key demographic variables.

Ideally, every survey question should be deliberate and explicitly linked to answering your research questions. You cannot ask a question for the sake of asking a question. Specifically, a good survey follows a standard protocol: your research questions (or subquestions) should be informed by your literature review, which will determine how you ask a particular question. In turn, the answer to that question on the survey will simply and logically inform the results to your research question. Figure 5.4 provides a visual representation of this explicit linkage between research questions and survey questions.

If, for example, you are interested in the relationship between principals' leadership styles and teachers' morale, the research literature may suggest that an important proxy is examining how teachers feel about "school culture," or that the demographic makeup of the local community and student body may matter. Your survey should thus ask about school culture (there are numerous well-respected studies and surveys that evaluate this), and the answers, in turn, will inform how you analyze your larger research question.

This process, though, is much easier said than done. It is difficult to create a neutral, valid, and reliable survey. This is why I strongly advise my students to use their literature reviews as a means for strengthening their own research design. There is no need to reinvent the wheel. If you are examining teacher relationships across racial and ethnic lines, there are probably several well-done and highly cited studies already on the issue that used some type of survey methodology. Most academic books and journal articles provide some or all of the survey questions. The point is not to simply cut and paste these questions into your study. (You would first, of course, have to get the researchers' permission anyway.) The point is to understand why the researchers asked the research questions that they did. Usually, this is discussed in the theoretical framework and methodology sections, just like it should be in your dissertation. The researchers probably explained why they used the questions that they did and how these questions link to the issue they are studying. Knowing this allows you to decide whether you can use their survey questions as is, modify them for your specific context, or realize that they are not applicable.

Irrespective of the level of modification, be clear that your survey questions are grounded in your own literature review, which itself is grounded in the research questions of your study. Having this explicit thread will

**Figure 5.4** From Research Questions to Survey Questions

Your research question should drive the research study. For survey research, this means that you are investigating particular hypotheses (whether tentative or formal) that are grounded in a particular literature. As such, each and every survey question should be directly linked back to a specific research question, which itself is grounded in and related to specific literature. The visual below represents this relationship as well as a part of one student's formalization of these linkages in her own survey.

Hypothesis

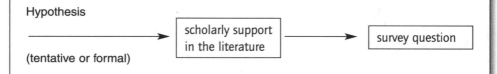

(tentative or formal)

*Student example:*

**Research Question # 4:** What aspects of job satisfaction are most important to the preretirement teacher?

**Item Number, Statement, and Source**

- # 4. I am treated as a professional. (B)
- # 6. I have the support and respect of my colleagues. (B)
- # 12. Teachers are trusted to make sound professional decisions about instruction. (C)
- # 13. Teachers have a role in determining the content of in-service professional development programs. (C)
- # 14. There is an atmosphere of trust and mutual respect in the school. (C)
- # 15. The school leadership actively supports teachers. (C)
- # 18. I would choose teaching again as a career. (A)

*Note:* Sources for this figure are as follows:

A = Researcher created this question.

B = This item is from the *School Participant Empowerment Survey* (2003).

C = This item is from the *Teachers Working Conditions Survey* (1998).

make your data analysis simple, logical, and powerful. You'll be able to show how the results of particular survey questions directly inform your findings regarding particular research questions. Moreover, such findings will be linkable to the research literature and can be examined in relationship to the past surveys from the studies you cited in the literature review.

Another key point is that the demographic variables are critical because they allow you to disaggregate your findings. Just like the analysis of the preexisting data in the previous section and the disaggregating your idea from Chapter 3, an important part of your analysis now rests on teasing out and controlling for the mediating variables. Perhaps new teachers had different perspectives than older teachers; perhaps male and female students had fundamentally different views about their friends; perhaps Hispanic parents were more prone to disagree with a policy than white parents. In fact, the seemingly innocuous questions that come at the beginning of a survey—gender, ethnicity, age, etc.—can oftentimes be the most important ones. If you don't ask, you will never know.

This does not mean you should ask every single potential mediating variable under the sun. It probably, for example, won't help to disaggregate your data based on who likes vanilla versus chocolate ice cream. But, again, the literature review exists to help you narrow down the potential key mediating variables and then incorporate them into your survey. The literature review thus becomes doubly important in survey research exactly because once you've collected the data, there is almost no way to go back and re-ask new questions. A survey that does not ask just one or two key questions—whether these are demographic or research based—may turn out to be worthless.

It is, therefore, extremely helpful to test your survey. This can be done informally with friends sitting around the dinner table, or more formally through an actual pilot study, given to a random sample of individuals who typify the population you want to survey. Figure 5.5 provides a modified example of a pilot survey done by one of my doctoral students. The survey is a good first draft: it has an opening statement such that the readers can understand why they are taking the survey; it is short, allowing it to be done quickly; it is composed solely of closed-ended questions, again supporting the timeliness of completion and ease of data coding; it has a good range of demographic variables that appear relevant; and the research questions appear neutrally phrased, avoiding potential bias.

Interestingly, my student received some excellent feedback that helped with the final distributed survey: individuals recommended the survey should be translated into Spanish on the reverse side (he was surveying a predominantly immigrant population); he should include his name and contact information as a way to support accountability and follow-up questions; there was concern as to whether some of the questions were repetitive and really got at the issues he was interested in (forcing him to go back to his literature review to confirm the alignment between the

**Figure 5.5**  Survey Sample

Dear [    ]:

Please take a moment to complete this survey. The answers that you provide will help a research study examining the potential of community "full-service schools." Your participation is voluntary. Information will be confidential. Your privacy will be protected and your name will not be shared with anyone.

Please provide the following information:

1. Your gender is (mark one answer):          ☐ male ☐ female

2. Check your ethnicity/race (mark all that apply):     ☐ White ☐ Black/African American ☐ Asian

     ☐ American Indian/Alaska Native

     ☐ Native Hawaiian/Other Pacific Islander

     ☐ Hispanic/ Latino (of any race)

3. Please fill in your age___

4. Were you born in the United States of America?  ☐ yes    ☐ no

5. Do you currently have children attending school? ☐ yes    ☐ no

*Please read the following definition of a "full-service school" carefully: Around the United States, full-service schools are places where families can get the help they need (health, mental health, social services) to support their children. School buildings are open before and after school, in the evenings, weekends, and during the summer. One or more community-based agencies partner with the schools.*

*Please circle the letters that shows how much you agree or disagree with the following statements*

*SA=strongly agree;  A=agree; D=disagree; SD=strongly disagree*

| | | | | |
|---|---|---|---|---|
| 1. My community needs more adult education and job training programs. | SA | A | D | SD |
| 2. My community needs more English as a Second Language programs. | SA | A | D | SD |
| 3. Schools in my community need to be more welcoming to parents and community members. | SA | A | D | SD |
| 4. Schools in my community need more programs for students with behavioral problems. | SA | A | D | SD |
| 5. Schools in my community should provide three free meals a day to students. | SA | A | D | SD |

*(Continued)*

(Continued)

| | | | | |
|---|---|---|---|---|
| 6. Schools in my community should provide three free meals to eligible community members. | SA | A | D | SD |
| 7. Nutrition education should be required of all students in school. | SA | A | D | SD |
| 8. Nutrition education should be available to members of the community. | SA | A | D | SD |
| 9. Schools in my community should require a "service project" before graduation. | SA | A | D | SD |
| 10. Schools should build relationships with organizations like the Boy Scouts, etc. | SA | A | D | SD |
| 11. Schools in my community need to work to promote "civic pride" in students. | SA | A | D | SD |
| 12. Schools and community agencies need to work more closely together. | SA | A | D | SD |
| 13. More health education needs to be provided to students. | SA | A | D | SD |
| 14. Health education should be available to members of the community. | SA | A | D | SD |
| 15. Schools should assist community members in understanding and filling out forms for assistance (i.e., WIC, SSI, etc.). | SA | A | D | SD |

research and his own study); and additional demographic variables were suggested, such as the primary language spoken at home, the grade level of the children, and the number of years individuals, if immigrants, had lived in the United States. My doctoral student now had an elegant and useful survey allowing him to gather key data on the surveyed population, and how their perspectives linked to his research questions. This allowed him to disaggregate the data across several key dimensions that facilitated a more nuanced understanding of the issue.

Survey creation is ultimately a complicated science that requires an understanding of issues ranging from population samples and response rates, to the value of open versus closed questions, and how to phrase questions neutrality. But if done right, surveys are extremely powerful tools to gather precise data.

## Interviews

Interviews are another popular research method in the social sciences to gather data. Much like surveys, they are a seemingly concrete and simple means for collecting key data from relevant individuals in an effective and controlled manner. The two most common modes of interviewing are one-on-one and focus groups. Irrespective of which type you conduct, it is important to note that just like surveys, interviewing is a complex undertaking that requires practice, thoroughness, and strict adherence to scholarly protocols. Given the numerous resources available (e.g., Seidman, 1998), two more general yet interrelated issues to keep in mind are the greater potential for interview bias and the need for good journalistic techniques.

Interviews have many of the same issues as surveys—such as the alignment of research questions to interview questions and the need for neutral phrasing. Interviews, though, have the added "wild card" variable of being done face-to-face. In some respects, this is extremely helpful because it allows you to note participants' body language and expressions, ask follow-up questions, and feel more personable about the entire process. Yet, these very same qualities can also contribute to not getting the data you really need. Researchers have long noted something called the "response effect bias," where people will tell interviewers what they want to hear. This is not to suggest people lie; it is simply that we modify our answers to be more socially acceptable and in general mute perspectives that are not culturally sanctioned. This is particularly true with complex and controversial matters. Researchers, moreover, have found that much depends on the interviewers: their gender, race and ethnicity, tone, and body language all impact how individuals answer the questions posed.

Because of this potential source of bias, it is critical to carefully structure your interview protocol. More specifically, effective interviewing asks open-ended questions that elicit meaningful and "deep" responses that take the shape of narratives. The last thing you want is to have people answer "yes" or "no" to your questions. That kind of "data" can be gathered through surveys. Rather, you want them to talk about their experiences, their feelings, and their intuitions surrounding the issue you are examining. Your job, as the researcher, will be to later transcribe and analyze the data, searching for patterns, themes, and distinctive perspectives. You can only do this if you have data "thick" enough to analyze. As such, think of yourself as a journalist trying to understand a story well enough to write about it. Interviews are your means to collect these stories—from students, teachers, parents, and principals—and then make sense of them.

Figure 5.6 presents a draft of one of my doctoral student's interview protocol. He was studying how a group of recent immigrants from an African country think about their identities as immigrants and how this affects their notions of education, citizenship, and sense of self. The interview protocol had some very nice features: it allowed him to ask standard questions with the opportunity for more open-ended follow-up; it explicitly had a place to jot notes about the interview as well as the interviewee's answers and mannerisms; it asked direct questions that were linked back to his research questions; and it was developed to be used over a period of

**Figure 5.6**    Interview Protocol Sample

| Interview Protocol (Questions to be covered during the six-month period) (partial list; modified) | | |
|---|---|---|
| **Questions** | **Note** | **Observation** |
| What does it mean to be [Nationality] to you? If individual unsure: Do you, for instance, still feel that you are a [Nationality]? That you are now an American? Or perhaps somewhere in between? | | |
| Follow-up: | | |
| To what degree do you feel [Nationality] immigrants maintain their cultural identity as they progress through the process of Americanization? If individual unsure: Do you feel that you have to "change" yourself now that you are here? | | |
| Follow-up: | | |
| Do you think some [Nationality] negotiate their identity? If so, to what degree? If individual unsure: Do you feel that some [Nationality] try to act differently? | | |
| Follow-up: | | |
| Do you think they are interested in integrating? Why or why not? | | |
| Follow-up: | | |

months such that he could see how, if at all, individuals changed their perspectives over time. In testing out the questions, though, he also realized that some of the questions were phrased too abstractly and were too closed-ended; that is, they prompted simple one-word responses. He thus had to change how he started his questions: from "Do you . . ." to "Tell me about. . . ."

The key is to figure out how to elicit a narrative from the person you are interviewing. Much of this may depend on subtle cues and prompts on your part: "Hmm . . . interesting." "Tell me more. . . ." "What exactly do you mean?" "Can you give me an example?" "Can you explain that again?" "What do you think others think about this?" Let them talk. The best way to scaffold such talk is to appear neutral and interested: ask open-ended questions about what you want to know, use a tape recorder so you can focus on the conversation, ask follow-up questions, and show that you are interested in what they are talking about. The deeper the discussion, the better your data will be.

## Document Analysis

Document analysis is a powerful yet oftentimes underused research strategy. This is especially true in exploratory research, case studies, and examinations of how well a program or intervention is working. Formally document analysis is the analysis of a text—with "text" being broadly understood as, for example, a physical document, a photograph, a movie, a Web site, a map, etc.—through a specific, standardized, and theoretically informed protocol (Hodder, 2003; Holsti, 1969). In other words, if you are examining a district's promotional materials, it cannot be done randomly without a clear sense of what you are looking for or why. Even an emergent design, based on the themes and patterns found along the way with seemingly no preconditions of what to look for, is "standardized" in the sense that there are very specific research assumptions for how the researcher needs to be open to discrepant cases, how to think about what is valid data, etc.

My sense is that document analysis is underused exactly because it appears so simple and "unscholarly." All of us, as teachers and administrators, use documents—handouts, reports, Web sites—each and every day. Our familiarity with documents thus seems to suggest that they are not worthy of inclusion in a research study. Yet, it is oftentimes the seemingly most familiar that is also the least examined. Texts are public documents. They are, whether we acknowledge it or not, the "face" and thus representation of the individual or organization that makes it public: the homework assignments I hand out in class, the way a district describes its soon-to-be-built high school, the affiliation of the individuals on a curriculum committee, the minutes of the board of higher education. All of these examples of texts can be fruitfully examined to glean key data relevant for your particular research study.

Good document analysis, just like surveys and interviews, has to be linked back to your research questions and the literature review that supported it. Moreover, your theoretical framework may be especially relevant here. If, for example, you are using a feminist lens, your document analysis may focus on the use of masculine wording, metaphors for teaching and learning as a competition, the particular use pronouns, etc. The style and substance of your document analysis should flow naturally from your research study and how you have framed it.

Because documents are in fact such a pervasive part of our lives, they can offer a wealth of unanticipated data. One of my doctoral students was able to use program documents as a key resource—in addition to interview and survey data—for determining whether and to what extent a set of newly formed small schools were meeting particular reform expectations. Figure 5.7 is a small part of a much larger matrix she developed that allowed her to see whether the collected program artifacts—newsletters, policy documents, e-mails, Websites—demonstrated achievement of particular "nonnegotiable" reform conditions, which, in this case, was the notion of autonomy and its subcomponents.

| Figure 5.7 | Program Artifacts Matrix Sample |

| Nonnegotiable Subcomponents | Leadership Academy | Lighthouse Academy | Technology Institute |
|---|---|---|---|
| 1. Autonomy | | | |
| Autonomous government | Disconfirmed | Disconfirmed | Disconfirmed |
| Budget | Confirmed | Confirmed | Confirmed |
| Structure | Confirmed | Confirmed | Confirmed |
| Staffing | Confirmed | Confirmed | Confirmed |
| Flexible use of resources | Confirmed | Confirmed | Confirmed |

To create such a matrix, my student used specific, predefined criteria and examined the literally hundreds of program documents from each school she was investigating. Much like an analysis of an interview transcript, she coded each document according to an emergent thematic system and then determined to what extent the documents demonstrated alignment to the specific criteria she was investigating. A school newsletter could thus have had important information about communication with parents, about the use of staff and resources, and about the relationship of that particular school with other local schools and the central administration. With enough documents and a clearly defined protocol, it is possible to develop a comprehensive picture of important issues across seemingly random and everyday documents.

## Field Observations

Conducting field observations—what anthropologists talk about as being "out in the field"—is probably the most time-intensive and least quantifiable mode of gathering data. It can also be the most rewarding in terms of gathering rich data. It offers the opportunity to see what is actually happening in specific situations rather than have someone tell you about it or provide a summary on a scale of one to five. Doing field observations can range from a very focused observation protocol used to conduct a school walk-through or classroom visit to something as open-ended as shadowing a principal for two months or sitting in the back of a cafeteria for an entire school year. Field observations are extremely useful for emergent designs that are exploratory in nature and that require a holistic perspective to begin to understand and work through the many nuanced and layered levels to a research situation (see, e.g., Burawoy, 1991; Merriam, 1998; Ragin & Becker, 2002). They are also a wonderful way to crosscheck data gathered by other means. I still remember my initial surprise when, after interviewing a teacher on his use of dynamic and interactive teaching strategies, I walked into his classroom to find nothing but lectures, worksheets, and student silence for an entire marking period.

The fundamental strength and weakness of gathering data through field observations is that the "researcher is the tool." Usually, you collect and analyze data through statistical analysis of existing data or through survey or interview questions. The data are already "packaged" in quantifiable ways (e.g., the only options on a survey could be strongly disagree, disagree, agree, and strongly agree) and can be analyzed through formalized procedures (e.g., looking for themes of leadership in the interview transcripts). In field-based research, though, anything and everything is directly filtered by you: Did you see what happened in the corner of the classroom? Should you take the principal's ironic tone seriously? Was she making a veiled threat to the new teachers? Did you catch what the student muttered under his breath? Real-time data collection is overwhelming exactly because you can't pause it, reanalyze it at your leisure, or ask the participants to just hold on a second so you can write this all down.

There are several ways to deal with this deluge of constant data. You could create a series of observation protocols that focus your observations: How many times do boys raise their hands? How often does the teacher ask questions versus just lecture? What percentage of faculty meetings is devoted to discussion? How often does the principal answer the phone and in what type of situations? Such focused and formalized protocols allow you to be precise in your data collection and avoid being overwhelmed by extraneous information. Alternatively, you could simply keep a detailed daily journal of impressions that, over time, come to display patterns of what catches your interest and focus. As such patterns emerge, you can focus your observations and writing on such situations and delve deeper into the contexts and ever-deeper examination of those moments. And, you could do a combination of the two. Some researchers, for example, set up a digital or audio recorder in an unobtrusive spot to record the "big picture" of what is happening in the entire classroom and, at the same time, sit in the other corner to focus on one specific ongoing process between two kids.

Irrespective of which method you use, field observations raise a host of methodological issues that are not as prevalent in other research methods. Since you are the "research tool," you have to do to yourself what you would have done for the survey or interview protocol; that is, you have to clarify and make transparent the limits and liability of the instrument. This is comparable to making sure that, for example, the survey questions are phrased neutrally. For field observations, this means clarifying your theoretical perspective, ensuring the validity of the process, and attending to the ethical dilemmas such observations may pose.

As discussed in Chapter 4, the world is not an obvious place, and neither is the way you look at it (Clifford & Marcus, 1986; Geertz, 1973). Our perspective is grounded in and clouded by the assumptions we hold, the worldview we ascribe to, and the language we use to discuss such things. Since you, the researcher, are the research instrument (as opposed to a survey or interview protocol), it becomes necessary for you to articulate the "lens" through which you are seeing the data. This does not mean some autobiographical introspection (though some researchers do in fact do this). It means clearly stating the framework within which you are examining the situations playing out in front of you. Are you watching classroom dynamics through a feminist lens (e.g., Sadker & Sadker, 1995)? Through the notion of sensemaking and storytelling (e.g., Weick, 1995)? Through a fourfold leadership framework (e.g., Bolman & Deal, 1991)? Articulating your dissertation's theoretical lens gives a clearer understanding of how observations are carried out and how the gathered data are subsequently analyzed.

Clarifying your theoretical perspective is also a necessary step toward enhancing the validity of your field observations. Such clarification informs the reader that your observations are not simply random and haphazard. They are done with purpose and consistency in mind; namely, your field observations are bound by a specific theoretical terminology that helps you look for and understand specific patterns and situations in a distinctive way. One's theoretical framework thus enhances validity. Validity—being sure of the strength and accurateness of one's conclusions—is necessary because it is seemingly harder to "prove" what is seen in the field if you are the only one doing the observations and conducting the analysis. There are no surveys to point to and no interview transcripts to cite—just your own "opinions" based on your observations. As such, field observations require a higher level of clarity regarding validity to convince the reader that you are doing a legitimate study that accurately represents what "really" happened. Your theoretical framework does exactly that.

You can also enhance your validity in field observations through a couple of standard practices (see Denzin & Lincoln, 2003). You can vary the "unit of analysis" of your observations, looking first, for example, at classroom dynamics and then observe just how the teacher interacts with girls; you can extend the length of your observations, whether that means the hours per day or the total number of days of observations; you can ask the individuals you are observing, called "member checking," whether you interpreted correctly the interactions you saw; and you can be conscious of and attendant to "discrepant cases" that help you to figure out whether what you are seeing is the norm.

The point to all of these validity-enhancing protocols is not to outline and detail your methodology such that another researcher can go in and "replicate" your findings. Qualitative research in general, and field observations in specific, don't abide by those rules. Rather, your goal is to enhance the trustworthiness of your research so you can describe and analyze your findings without having a skeptical and dubious reader over your shoulder. You can only do this by being clear about what you did, why you did it, and the limits and value of your methods. Just as you might attempt to show the trustworthiness of your survey questions by explaining their theoretical grounding and their linkage to the literature, you are doing the exact same thing about your own trustworthiness as the research tool.

The final issue regarding field observations is, implicit in this last example, the realization that a survey is a piece of paper and you are not. Put otherwise, there are numerous ethical issues that have to be attended to when you conduct field observations. A major issue that many of my doctoral students face is that their research is usually done in their "backyard." While there is nothing inherently wrong with such research, it raises a host of potentially thorny issues revolving around relationships with participants, insider bias, and impact from negative findings. Many of these issues are discussed subsequently with the IRB process, but they are critical aspects to consider. This is especially true if you will be doing any form of action research where you are not simply a "neutral" observer but an interested party and proponent for particular outcomes (see, e.g., Greenwood & Levin, 2007; Herr & Anderson, 2005).

## INSTITUTIONAL REVIEW BOARD (IRB)

In almost all of these research methods, you will be working with individuals, either youth or adults. You will, as such, need to go through your institution's Institutional Review Board (IRB). All research must go through an IRB committee to ensure that the research meets ethical guidelines and does not in any way impinge on the rights of the individuals being studied or harm them in any way. An IRB submission is necessary even if you are not directly working with human subjects, since the IRB can decide that a submission is "exempt" from review or should undergo an "expedited" or "full" review. These three categories are fairly well standardized across institutions and IRB committees, but you should always verify your institution's specific requirements and protocols with your advisor and proper administrative offices.

Dissertation research usually exempt from IRB review includes those that are working with public data sets (such as from the National Center for Educational Statistics [NCES]) as well as internal data sets that have no identifiable markers or where the researcher will not use such markers and thus deletes them from the data set. Additionally, your research may be exempt if it meets specific federal criteria as outlined in what is known as the Belmont Report and detailed in the federal Office for Human Research

Protections (OHRP), whereby the research is conducted in a "commonly accepted" educational setting involving "normal educational practices." One of the key criteria here is the level and amount of interaction and intervention with the individuals in the educational setting, whether that means students, teachers, or staff. Ask your advisor for support in figuring out the specifics and err on the side of being overly cautious as you develop your methodological protocols.

The distinction between an expedited and full review will be determined by the committee's balance of the potential risks to participants against the perceived benefits from the research. The IRB committee will think of "risk" in a very broad way, and therefore, so should you. Specifically, potential risks could include physical, psychological, legal, social, and economic risks. Participants, for example, could develop anxieties, be embarrassed by, or lose self-esteem based on your interview questions. If others knew about it, an individual participating in your survey could be stigmatized and labeled or suffer economic consequences such as the loss of a job. Finally, sensitive information gathered in your study about an individual could have legal and fiscal implications, such as a criminal or civil lawsuit. All of these risks are especially pronounced if you are working with "vulnerable" populations such as children or prisoners, and such research would usually fall under a full review.

There are, as such, a host of standard mechanisms and protocols that are expected and required both by research traditions and IRB committees. For example, the IRB committee will want to know the specific anticipated risks to participants and how you plan to minimize them, how confidentiality will be ensured, and that there is a clear and useful informed consent form that spells out the study. Figure 5.8 provides some of the key components of an IRB proposal; nevertheless, make sure that you follow the specifics of your particular institution.

Additionally, there are three specific things to keep in mind with your IRB submission: specificity, protection for participants, and minimizing conflicts of interest (see also Mertens, 2003; Miller, 2000; Oakes, 2002).

An IRB committee, just like your dissertation committee, wants to know as much as possible about how you will collect your data: What data will you collect? Through what methodology? How many times? What questions will you ask? The IRB committee wants to make sure that there is clarity around the process, so they can be assured that there are no inadvertent slipups or sensitive situations you may not have thought about.

Fundamentally, the IRB is set up to protect the participants in your study. Participants are doing you a favor by being a part of your study, and the last thing you want is to harm them in any way. Part of this protection is fairly standard: you want to maintain confidentiality of the data gathered and anonymity of the individuals participating. Confidentiality refers specifically to the data gathered. You want to set up procedures to make sure that the data you gather will not inadvertently be made public. You

| Figure 5.8 | Key Components of an IRB Submission |

Make sure to follow the specific procedures of your institution. In general, these are the key parts of an IRB proposal and what you need to include.

1. **Proposal**. Focus on

   a. *Purpose of investigation and procedures:* Provide a brief statement about the background, objectives, research methods, and scholarly merit of the study.

   b. *Anticipated risk and potential benefits:* Describe the potential risk and benefits faced by participants. Risks include physical, psychological, social, legal, or economic harm. Describe why the relationship between the risks and benefits of the study are reasonable and the importance of the knowledge that will result. *Note: Course credit, payment, and vague benefits to society are not considered benefits to the participant.*

   c. *Steps taken to protect participants:* Describe the process by which participants' will be protected against any risks and how their confidentiality, if applicable, will be protected, including the collecting and storing of data.

   d. *Manner of obtaining participants:* Describe the process by which participants will be recruited. If particular populations are targeted, such as children or one ethnic group, explain the rationale. Also explain the consent procedures to be used and any plans for compensation.

2. **Statement of Informed Consent:** Please attach an unsigned form, using a standardized format and style. This should include, at minimum, a description of the research purpose, procedures, and any foreseeable risks and benefits. It should also detail the procedures in place to minimize risk, insure confidentiality to the extent possible, and ability to opt out of the study. Finally, it should have the contact information of the researcher, the researcher's dissertation advisor, and the IRB committee of the institution.

3. **Debriefing Statement:** This form is to be used only if the informed consent form does not provide a full explanation of the study. When deception or manipulation is used, a debriefing form is required.

4. **Research Materials:** You should attach—either as appendices or in the body of the proposal—all of the relevant materials to be used in your research. This may include surveys, interview questions, or a classroom observation protocol form. Make sure you cite your sources.

should, for example, keep all data on a personal computer rather than on a work computer that may be publically accessible; you should set up a password for your personal computer (all computers have this feature, usually in the "administrative tools" section of your control panel); you should keep your notebooks, filled-in surveys, interview transcripts, etc., at home in a locked filing cabinet; and you should clearly state in your methodology that you will not use, discuss, or benefit from the data gathered for the research at work, with colleagues, or any other public venue without the informed consent of the individuals providing you with such data. You do not want someone to wander by your office and see that a specific teacher said so-and-so about the principal in your field notes.

Whereas confidentiality refers primarily to the data you are collecting, anonymity refers primarily to how you present these data in your dissertation. A basic model for anonymity is to create pseudonyms for the individuals interviewed or the schools studied. Additionally, it may be necessary to take this anonymity to the next level by not revealing or slightly modifying the characteristics of the individual (perhaps changing their grade levels or gender) or the location of the school (such as simply stating that it is in the southern half of a western state). The key at this stage is to make sure that what you do not reveal or modify is minimally relevant information for your dissertation: you don't want, for example, to change the gender of an individual to safeguard identity if your dissertation is exploring issues of gender in the curriculum. This process will thus be a delicate balancing act, and you should have the help of your dissertation committee with these decisions.

Another aspect of anonymity, especially with survey and interview data, is to be careful in the disaggregation process. It may so happen, for example, that out of 200 returned surveys, there is only one African American, male, elementary teacher. It would thus be inappropriate to present data at that level of specificity. You could simply talk about elementary teachers' perspectives, or about male teachers' perspective, but as soon as the population of potential individuals in any particular category falls below a certain threshold, you need to rethink how you present these data.

On a deeper level, it is important to realize that protection for participants goes beyond confidentiality and anonymity. Your statement of informed consent, for example, should have a standard phrase that gives participants the ability to opt out of the study at any time, and, moreover, to have their data deleted from your dissertation altogether. While this may be a hassle for you if it does in fact occur, it could be devastating to a person's career if particular information becomes public. The informed consent form should also have the contact information for you and your advisor in case the individual wants to contact one or both of you with questions, concerns, or complaints. It is usually a good idea to also develop a feedback mechanism (whether formal or informal) concerning the data you collect from an individual. Some researchers do it through the formal "member check" whereby they relate back to the individual the kind of data they are hearing; others informally give individuals a rough draft of the sections written about them. The point in both cases is that the participating individuals have input and thus partial control over how they are presented. This does not mean that they can veto your analysis and conclusions. It simply means that their perspectives are heard more clearly and they are given the ability to correct the record, if so necessary.

Finally, note that what we may think of as innocuous or really minor data and information can be a bombshell for someone else. You may think it is irrelevant, for example, that a principal noted that she was not at a certain central-office meeting when a decision was being made about bussing routes. But the superintendent may be incensed to learn that a particular staff member did not invite the principal to that critical meeting. While there is no simple or surefire way to scrub a dissertation clean of controversial material—and in fact your dissertation may have the controversial material at the heart of the dissertation argument—it is critical that you show the IRB committee, and by implication the individuals you are hoping will partici-pate in your study, that you will go through the due diligence of setting up specific protocols and processes to insure that sensitive information is not revealed. One way to achieve this, though it is not common, is for a disser-tation to be "embargoed" (the technical term for withholding public access to a dissertation for a period anywhere from six months to ten years). Whatever route you take, realize that assurances backed up with in-place protocols will ease the anxiety of everyone, including you.

A final focus for the IRB committee is the potential for conflict of inter-est. Exactly because educators focus their dissertations on issues that can support their own work in their specific situations, a common problem, touched upon earlier, is "backyard research" (Creswell, 2003). Many of my doctoral students, simply through the sheer pragmatics of being in a par-ticular district with limited access to other schools or districts, do their research among their colleagues. Technically, this is known as a conve-nience sampling; while there is nothing fundamentally wrong with this, it raises a host of ethical and methodological problems that should be addressed in the methodology and, especially, for the IRB committee.

An example of such a problem occurred when one of our doctoral students—a principal of an urban school—wanted to study the opportu-nities for, and challenges to, the development of "learning communities" among his elementary and middle school teachers. While this was a fasci-nating and important topic, it raised numerous red flags for his disserta-tion committee: as the principal, he had oversight and power over his teachers across multiple areas, from assigning committee work to profes-sional evaluations. Moreover, as a long-standing principal, he had a his-tory at the school, with all of the positive and negative implications for interaction patterns, long-held grudges, favors made and given, etc. How would he collect data without biasing the responses? Would teachers simply tell him what he wanted to hear? What if he discovered a problem with a teacher in the course of the study? Could he act on it or did it have to remain confidential? Could a teacher really opt out of the study with no negative ramifications?

What we recommended, and what the IRB committee ultimately approved, was a highly focused study that aligned with his day-to-day responsibilities as a school principal. Data were gathered from historical and current records (document analysis), through anonymous Web-based surveys with minimal identifying demographic variables, and reflective journaling based on his already-accepted duties (classroom visitations, leading faculty meetings, etc.) This design minimized forced interactions with faculty that did not constitute standard operating procedure and allowed both faculty and the principal to maintain their professional duties.

## SOME FINAL THOUGHTS BEFORE "ABD-LAND"

Ultimately, no research is perfect. And neither is any single research tool. Even in combination, all research tools have limits to the data they can "capture" and accurately depict. There are pragmatic reasons for such limitations: for example, there is not enough time in the field; it is unethical to probe beyond a certain point or in regard to certain issues. There are theoretical limitations as well: How exactly do we know what people think about something if they themselves are not clear on it? Is it even possible to capture and accurately quantify subtle gestures that make all the difference between two meanings of that gesture? The anthropologist Clifford Geertz (1973) offered a classic example of the uncertainty between knowing whether someone just winked at you or simply had something in her eye. Or, perhaps, she meant to be ironic and exaggerate the wink but got something in her eye at the very moment she was attempting to wink. How do we know?

Geertz, following Ryle (1971), offered the heuristic of "thick description" as a means to partially overcome this analytical problem. But ultimately, Geertz suggested, all of our interpretations are built upon the stories we tell and the multiple valences to such stories. There is no singular and objective truth that can be found, for each seemingly concrete level of interpretation ("she said she winked") is itself resting on top of other interpretations ("maybe she said that because she saw me looking at her"); in other words, it's interpretation all the way down.

With this in mind, all that you can do in your dissertation is accept that your goal is not to find the "true" bottom; it is instead to be as transparently clear as possible about which stories you are telling, why you are telling them, and how they are told. Since you cannot prove everything, much less one thing, conclusively, all you can do is set up a strong, logical, and thorough study in order to analyze your particular topic. Even multimillion dollar, federally funded, multiyear projects with many researchers cannot come to definitive conclusions. You, as a single researcher over some months, cannot hope to duplicate federal initiatives. The solution is not to try or to give up. It is to be extremely focused, precise, and honest. Clearly articulating your limitations is in fact the greatest gift you can give yourself. When questioned about tangential issues related to your topic, you can easily and honestly state that this was not a part of your research design or theoretical focus. It can be an excellent follow-up study, but it is not your study. That can be, as I always quip to my overly ambitious students, your next dissertation.

So, you've written up your proposal, submitted your IRB, and developed your bibliography. That's it. Submit your materials; sit back and wait a few weeks. Once you're approved, it's time to collect and analyze the data, and then begin to write about it.

# 6

## *Putting It All Together*

### *Completing Your Dissertation*

There is a seemingly gaping hole, a vast chasm, between the previous page and this one. In one moment, I was wishing you well on having your dissertation proposal approved, and in the next moment, I am assuming and expecting that you are ready to start putting your dissertation draft all together. How did we get here? And why did we skip through all of the actual "stuff"—data collection and analysis—that is supposed to be at the heart of the dissertation? The answer is that you have to understand the end of the process before you can start at the beginning. This is as true for the overall process as it is for the data collection and analysis. You have to understand why you are gathering data and what you will do with it in order to understand which data to collect and how to analyze them.

This chapter shows you what is necessary to actually complete the dissertation such that you can then—even as you are just beginning data collection and analysis—know how to think about your data collection and analysis strategies. This chapter thus does not provide specific strategies for collecting and analyzing your data. This is not only because every dissertation topic and issue is slightly different and unique. Rather, even though every dissertation topic may indeed be unique, there is in fact a very standardized format for writing about such data and a highly delimited protocol to make sure that your dissertation does this correctly. This chapter provides you with this structure and the protocol to get there, and ideas for how to mold your own data into shape. By the end of this chapter you should see how any and every quality dissertation follows a similar pattern and structure, so that you can do so as well, even though you may have just started the process.

This commonality of a standard format is, by the way, just as true for a good Broadway play as it is for a gripping detective novel or a dissertation. While there are exceptions to this rule—Samuel Beckett's famous play, *Breath*, for example, was twenty-five seconds long and featured nothing other than a pile of rubbish on stage and a recorded baby's cry—such outliers presume (and play against) the standard of a tradition. For example, the philosopher Jacques Derrida brought forth a host of profound revisions in the 1970s to how scholars thought about and analyzed texts. His books (e.g., 1976, 1978) displayed anomalous modes of writing that upended much of the philosophical world. Yet, when one examined other academics writing about Derrida, they bore very little trace of such types of writing. The academic analysis was, for the most part, traditional. What this suggests is that while it may be fine for academic luminaries to write in nonstandard ways, a dissertation should be deeply standard. A dissertation should display a working knowledge and mastery of the standard academic traditions. This is why one can think of the dissertation as a machine.

## THE DISSERTATION AS A "MACHINE"

The first draft of a dissertation is never a pretty document. That's why it's called a first draft. The question, though, is how do you move from a first or even a second draft to a final draft? What constitutes "final," and what does it look like? To be even more precise, how do you begin to link all of the chapters, ideas, and threads together? The short and simple answer is that a dissertation should "flow"; it should be a story that can be read from start to finish just like any other narrative, with a coherent plotline and a beginning, middle, and an end. Again, what exactly does that mean?

It means that the dissertation, just like a good story, is logically and deliberately linked. The raising of questions, themes, or research should all be done for a purpose, in that sooner or later the story/ dissertation returns back to explain, contrast, or build upon the key and central questions and issues. A good narrative does not introduce a character and then simply drop him from the script. A good story provides a "red thread" such that the reader can follow the narrative buildup, understand where specific ideas came from, and trace how they develop across the entire dissertation. You don't want to close a good book and ask yourself, "So what exactly happened to the main character?" or "Why did the author raise those points?" The lack of "loose threads" in quality literature makes vivid that a narrative has to be precise in its machinery. This is what I term the "dissertation as machine."

The "dissertation as machine" metaphor suggests that once the mechanisms start turning, they go through a self-enclosed, self-sufficient, and eminently predictable procedure. This gear turns that winch, which drops that bearing into that slot, which opens this door, etc. And, if desired, one could actually write out all of these procedures and see the entire process in a single and simple schematic diagram. While, of course, neither the dissertation nor the dissertation process actually occurred like that, neither did a brilliant book begin brilliant, nor a piece of machinery function as anticipated. Each had to be plotted, revised, and reconfigured numerous times. But once complete, an external reader would never know such "behind the scenes" back-and-forth. All she would see is an elegant process that appears obvious, simple, and self-explanatory. Figure 6.1 maps what your dissertation should look like when it is complete and seemingly "obvious."

The first chapter provides the reader with the "big picture" of why this dissertation research was undertaken in the first place. You have to answer the reader's "so what?" question to the satisfaction of why this is a meaningful topic and what you can add to the discussion. This means that you should summarize the main issues and debates in the literature, which will be expanded upon in much more depth in chapter two. For now, though, this summary explains the relevance and scope of your study and in turn informs the meaningfulness and validity of the actual research questions. These research questions are themselves informed already—though the reader doesn't know this yet—by the literature review, since the literature review demonstrates why you have phrased and focused the research questions as you have. Thus, what first simply appears as good research questions, given the context and problem already described, becomes much more relevant and meaningful once the reader gets deeper into the literature review in chapter two.

The second chapter should thus appear as a natural and logical consequence of the articulated context and specific research questions. This chapter should provide a detailed description and analysis of each seemingly relevant literature strand that has bearing on the research question. I usually advise my students that there should be anywhere between three and five strands. Every educational issue is a "wicked problem" impacted by a potentially vast number of variables, and, as such, requires nuanced examination. If you have just one or two strands, you risk missing a key aspect of the problem. If you have more than five strands, you risk opening the lens too wide and thus analyzing everything under the sun. Chapter one should have specified the limitations of the study, and these limitations can now be seen by which strands are and are not examined. Each strand, in turn, should provide key insights

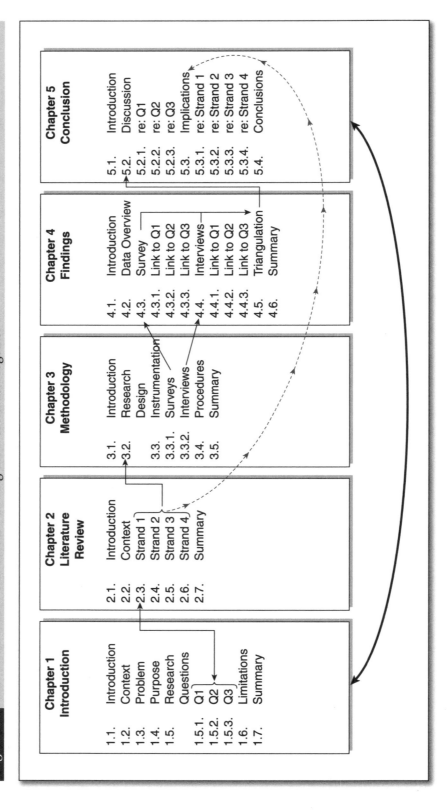

**Figure 6.1** The "Dissertation as Machine": Linking the Dissertation Together

about your specific research question and used in the next chapter to guide the actual data collection.

Using the context of your particular research question, chapter three should now intuitively build upon the research examined in the previous chapter. If previous researchers used a particular survey or interview method, for example, you may also use it, albeit with minor modifications for your particular school population. If previous researchers realized the limitations of a specific intervention, then perhaps your research design will examine this specific gap, or follow-up with a modified design to capture that missing data. If one group of researchers found a specific curriculum as the key and another group of researchers found a specific instructional style as the key, perhaps your research will examine both the curriculum and instructional style to determine how the two interact. Chapter three, then, builds on what others have done and articulates the very specific methods by which you intend to conduct your study in your specific context. Likewise, the seemingly "abstract" literature review now becomes visible (i.e., operationalized) through the particular data-collection tools—be they surveys, interview questions, or observation protocols.

Chapter four should logically follow as nothing more than a descriptive and analytical articulation and analysis of the data you found through the procedure outlined in the previous chapter. You can organize the data by research question, instruments used, or by the data themselves. The key is to present the data gathered that bear directly upon the research questions asked in the first chapter. The data should come easily and simply from each data collection tool and be analyzed in light of the research questions. Since this chapter is simply about the gathered data, it should logically close with a concluding analysis (i.e., triangulation) that examines all of the data in relation to each other.

The fifth chapter serves as a bookend to the dissertation. It should simply take the concluding analysis from the previous chapter and discuss how the findings inform the original research questions. Having done this, chapter five can also explore the larger academic context of how the research fits into and informs the ongoing discussions in the literature and, in turn, impacts our understanding of the bigger picture of that specific issue. Finally, having answered the specific research questions and explaining how this study fits into the larger academic context, chapter five should conclude with suggestions and implications of future analyses, given what has now been learned; that is, knowing now the outcomes of this study, what would be the logical next step in examining that particular issue? Other researchers can now build upon what you have done.

To summarize this entire process, your goal—albeit a really high goal—is that once the reader reads the title, the dissertation more or less "writes itself." The title should suggest the research questions, which in turn suggest the larger context and the literature review that supports understanding the questions; the literature review informs the research design, which creates the parameters for the kind of data gathered and analyzed; the description and analysis of the findings, in turn, return to the main research questions in order to develop conclusions that link your findings to the existing literature and the larger context of the original problem, that is, why the dissertation research was begun in the first place. You're done. That was easy.

Except, of course, it wasn't. For what I have just articulated in a seemingly linear and chronological process could not have been possible without an extremely detailed reverse-chronological procedure. Car companies will buy a competitor's car and take it apart bit by bit until all that is left is the thousands and thousands of pieces. This process of "reverse engineering" allows them to understand how and why their competitors built their cars the way they did. Similarly, you will now have to reverse engineer your dissertation.

To explain this to my doctoral students, I first ask them, "Why do birds fly south in the winter?" and then answer my own question: "Because it's too far to walk. . . ." After my students finish groaning at the joke, I tell them that there's actually a fundamental point here. A joke doesn't work unless the joke-teller knows the punch line before he begins the joke. The beginning is one big setup to the forthcoming punch line. And that too is the key to a good dissertation. It is one big setup to the concluding chapter. I am not suggesting that you should reinforce your preexisting assumptions or predrawn conclusions. Rather, after working hard to examine and reexamine your data and analysis, you now need to put it all together in a meaningful and impactful way.

This is hard to accomplish, just like it is hard to pull off what appears to be an effortless joke; the joke-teller has to first know the punch line and then work backward to figure out a good setup. This is the same with a dissertation. The problem with most dissertations (and most research in general) is that we all write linearly, that is, chapter by chapter. The key to realize is that when you are done with your linear write-up, you have really just written the first full draft of your dissertation. Don't send this to your dissertation chair. What you now need to do, now that you have gotten to the end and realized your "punch line," is go back and revise each and every chapter, starting with the first chapter, keeping this punch line in mind.

## REVERSE ENGINEERING YOUR DISSERTATION

Reverse engineering your dissertation means with the conclusion beginning and walking backward through each chapter to make sure that each claim and argument is supported by the research that came beforehand. Figure 6.2

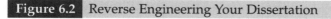

**Figure 6.2**    Reverse Engineering Your Dissertation

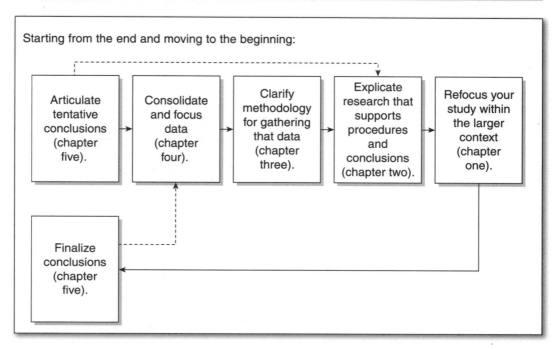

provides a schematic of this process and is in many ways just a simple reversal of Figure 6.1. You most likely already have some tentative conclusions based on your initial analysis and synthesis of the data. Additionally, living with these data and this study for so long, you likely have a "feel" for what will support these conclusions. Moreover, all of the relevant data for your dissertation are themselves probably part of a much larger pile of raw data, journal notes, and documentation that are compiled in a not yet fully coherent and logical order. Put otherwise, your first dissertation draft is ready to be carefully and systematically tightened up through a reverse-engineering process.

The tentative conclusions in chapter five can, for now, be as simple as jottings, bullet points, and random and key ideas you have had throughout the dissertation process. I encourage my students to write down any and all conclusions, implications, and ideas for future research in chapter five and simply let it all "brew" as they continue with their writing, analyzing, and synthesis. To ensure a point of departure for the forthcoming revision, choose four or five of what you consider to be the key conclusions (you can always add or subtract more later) and use these as the basis for reviewing chapter four.

Based on these chosen conclusions, examine the triangulation or concluding analytic section of chapter four to see whether your data support such conclusions. In turn, trace each of your data points back to the descriptive sections at the beginning of chapter four as well as the analysis of that data. You will most likely find that some of your conclusions do not have any or minimal data behind them, or, alternatively, you may have lots of data that don't seem to lead to any conclusion.

You must now work within chapter four to make sure that all of these threads are aligned. Figure 6.3 outlines the four basic scenarios that you will encounter with your data and conclusions and what should be done: (1) if you have both strong conclusions and strong data support, simply edit these sections to make them flow well; (2) if you have conclusions that you know are strong but currently have minimal data support, either find data that support such conclusions (and thus expand the descriptive write-up and analytic examination of them) or drop both the data and the conclusions; (3) if you have conclusions that appear weaker and also have minimal data support, delete both that data from chapter four and the conclusions from chapter five; and (4) if you have strong data with minimal linkage to any conclusions, expand your write-up of the final section in chapter four to support new and expanded conclusions in chapter five.

**Figure 6.3**  Aligning Data and Conclusions

|  |  | Conclusions | |
|---|---|---|---|
|  |  | *Strong* | *Weak* |
| **Data** | *Strong* | Make minor edits. | Expand and create conclusions. |
|  | *Weak* | Find data to support such conclusions or drop the conclusions and thus the data. | Drop conclusions and data. |

This recursive process in chapter four, it should be noted, should foster additional thinking about, and revision of, conclusions and implications for chapter five. Expect and embrace these insights, for it is not until now, as you reach the end of the process, that your dissertation should be finally coming together for you. What at first appeared as random or semi-related points or threads should now begin to make sense, and become firmer and clearer. As new conclusions emerge, they need to be traced back to chapter four to confirm that the data exist to support their inclusion.

Once the data in chapter four appear to support the conclusions in chapter five, move backward to chapter three to make sure that the methodology actually describes the data you have just written about. Did, for example, you actually use the data from the first set of surveys or was that taken out? Did you explain how you gathered the documents that you have now added to buttress your arguments in chapter four? You will most likely need to remind yourself of where data came from and how they were gathered. Make sure, again, that every bit of data discussed in chapter four is clearly talked about in chapter three; and, likewise, all methodology that does not link directly to data in chapter four should be removed. You do not want the reader to all of a sudden stumble upon data in chapter four with no sense from chapter three of how they were gathered.

Chapter two is the only chapter that cannot simply be reverse engineered. This is because the reverse engineering, in a sense, already occurred at the proposal stage when you moved back and forth between chapters one and two to create your research questions. Nevertheless, there are two components of chapter two that should undergo this same type of process to make sure it is aligned with the rest of the dissertation. First, chapter two should show how the methodology in chapter three is found in the literature review. If you used a specific survey or interview protocol, chapter two should discuss how and why other researchers have used such methodological tools that, in turn, informed your own use of it. Alternatively, if you developed your own research tools to gather data, chapter two should clearly show how and why you developed and framed these research tools; that is, why were specific questions asked and why were they phrased as they were? Again, the reader should never be surprised to come upon a research tool in chapter three that was not first discussed either implicitly or explicitly in the previous chapter.

The second means to align chapter two relates to the conclusions in chapter five. All of the conclusions in chapter five should have some relationship to the literature review in chapter two. This relationship does not have to be explicit in chapter two for each and every forthcoming conclusion. You may, for example, discover that what was originally viewed as a minor variable in the literature has come to dominate your research study. Nevertheless, just like with the methodology chapter, chapter two should introduce every key issue that will ultimately be in chapter five. And, likewise, any literature review that does not directly relate to what is ultimately discussed in chapter five should be either dropped or significantly cut.

Let us pause for a moment to reflect on this last point: namely, that I have been suggesting throughout this process that you unceremoniously cut many parts of your dissertation. You likely spent a substantial amount of time on these sections, and you also may feel that each and every section is critical and important, even if it does not directly relate to your dissertation. This is a difficult moment in the dissertation process because you are being advised to throw away a good portion of your hard work. And unfortunately, this is true. The big-picture point that needs to be reiterated is that a first draft is just a first draft. Just like an author probably cut a character or a tangential plot development in order to craft a tighter and more powerful story, so too must you cut sections that do not align with or ultimately support your final conclusions.

You can, though, save the deleted sections in another document and return to them to develop them in other ways, such as a conference paper or article. But if they do not fit into the framework of your dissertation, they should not be included. To present this as a some-what more high-stakes scenario, you don't want to spend your disser-tation defense attempting to explain why you have included data with no conclusions or a literature review about an issue that does not appear in the rest of the dissertation. Everything you are doing now, in this reverse-engineering process, is about passing your dissertation defense. All of your other ideas, research, and literature review may be wonderful. Just don't confuse this with the task of writing a good— and passable—dissertation.

Finally, once chapter two reflects both the upcoming methodology and ultimate conclusions, you can return to your first chapter. You must now bring all of the threads together so that the reader begins reading what appears to be a fascinating and coherent narrative. Your statement and contextualization of the research problem should presage the literature review that is forthcoming; your phrasing of the research questions should clearly link to the research tools used to gather the necessary data to answer such questions; your overview of the dissertation should mirror what will actually come up in the forthcoming chapters. Thus, as sug-gested earlier, once the reader begins chapter one, the rest of the narrative should flow smoothly and directly from this initial setup.

The process I have just described, I should caution, cannot be achieved in a single run-through. Once you have done this process one time, you will most likely need to revisit what you have written in chap-ter five. The process most likely also generated new ideas for conclusions and implications as well as linkages to the literature. As such, you should be prepared that this run-through may need to be repeated one, or even two, more times. Each time, it will be tighter and hopefully easier to do. Think of the second and third times as fine-tuning whereas the first time was a major overhaul. Once this is done, you should have a strong and coherent dissertation.

## WHAT ARE THE REMAINING KEY ISSUES?

Above and beyond the fundamental work of writing up a strong draft, there are some additional minor and major points to be aware of. While all of these points are either implicitly or explicitly part the process described in the previous section, it is helpful to separate them out for further clari-fication. This will give you an additional sense of what to think about as you put your dissertation draft together.

### Triangulating Data

Data triangulation is the cross-referencing and synthesis of multiple data sources in order to enable more valid analysis and conclusions. Data triangulation is not always necessary, since long-term observations, in-depth interviews, and multiple surveys can also accomplish the same goal of collecting valid data. Nevertheless, if data about a particular reform effort can be gained from multiple sources, such as document analysis, interviews, and surveys, they add a stronger foundation upon which to draw conclusions.

The triangulation of data does not mean that there has to be agreement across data sources. In fact, some of the most fruitful and important findings may occur when data sources actually conflict with each other. For example, teacher surveys may show strong support for a particular curricular reform effort; yet, in interviews, teachers may actually voice doubts about it, and classroom observations may find that such curricular tools are not even used. It is not that there is something "wrong" with some of the data. Rather, different research tools reveal different perspectives. One of the fundamental conclusions may be that while there is rhetorical support for a curricular reform, such rhetoric does not translate into actual practice. This is a potentially powerful finding. Don't, as such, hide or ignore contradictory findings; instead, confirm that your data do indeed demonstrate such contradictory perspectives and then examine how and why such differences may exist.

## Using Your Own Voice

My doctoral students consistently ask me about when they can use their "own" voice in the dissertation. Your own voice, I tell them, should only come out in the final chapter when you discuss your conclusions and implications. This is, of course, an oversimplification since you are the one who writes the dissertation, makes the decisions about what should and should not be included, and analyzes and synthesizes the data. Your voice is all over the dissertation. Nevertheless, this is your voice only in the sense that you are the author; my students are instead referring to "voice" as an individual "outside" of the dissertation who has her own perspectives, ideas, and feelings above and beyond the specific data and context of the dissertation. "When," they are basically asking, "can I just say what I want to say?" My answer is that this is not really appropriate in a dissertation outside of the concluding sections of chapter five.

Your dissertation is a systematic examination of a particular topic. There is literally no space (or need) for opinions or feelings that are not a part of this systematic process. This is just as true of a qualitative dissertation as a quantitative dissertation. A qualitative dissertation is different in that the "researcher is the instrument" and the reader needs to understand your perspectives, conceptual approach, and potential biases much more clearly. Nevertheless, this does not mean that you can simply or casually present your opinions; you still have to write the dissertation according to academic protocols of good qualitative research, which includes clarity, trustworthiness, and constant attention to not biasing the study. Once you pass the dissertation defense, you are free to advocate a particular opinion or perspective as much as you want. But the dissertation is about the data, not you.

## Answering Your Research Questions

This may sound silly, but many dissertations never really end up answering their own initial research questions. The dissertation takes turns and twists and, before you know it, concludes on some interesting results that may not be directly linked to the questions at the beginning of the dissertation. Or, more problematically, the dissertation may veer off track, given the lack of recursive back-and-forth between the research question, data, and analysis. As such, make sure you return to your initial questions and answer them. On one level, your dissertation chair is responsible for making sure that you have indeed answered the research questions that framed and guided your study. Nevertheless, as the reverse-engineering process should have clearly shown, your conclusions should flow directly from the research questions. Make sure they do so.

## Finding No Finding

It is often the case that a research study concludes with a negative finding: for example, the intervention produced no measureable positive results. Formally, this is known as proving the null hypothesis, which is the opposite of what one is hoping to find. This lack of a positive finding can be a difficult and frustrating dilemma. You may feel that you now have nothing to report (assuming that gathering more data is not an option or has already been attempted). What do you do?

Do not confuse the negative results of your study with the belief that you do not have adequate data to answer your research questions. You do have enough data. It just so happens that the data are telling you that there are no positive findings. This is a legitimate conclusion that "no finding is a finding" (Ioannidis, 2005). Moreover, there may be numerous legitimate reasons for this outcome and important implications that can be derived from this "nonfinding." For example, future research may need to attempt the intervention in another way given that your model was not successful; your nonfinding may undercut previous literature or theories that presumed a positive outcome would occur; the limitations in the study (e.g., length of time) may reveal limits to the efficacy of the program being studied and cause revisions to be made. In all of these cases, your seemingly negative findings have numerous positive outcomes and implications. You just need to know how to express them.

## Remembering the Big Picture

Ultimately, you began your dissertation because you wanted to answer a fundamental question or probe a complex issue. Over the course of your dissertation, though, it is be very easy to lose sight of where you started and the passion you used to have. Now is the time to find it again. While a boring and quality dissertation will pass just as easily as an exciting and quality dissertation, no one wants to read a boring text. Remembering the big picture of why you started this process in the first place may help you to recapture the larger significance and answer the "so what?" question.

Additionally, I also suggest to students that they may want to include a short anecdote exactly about how this passion or interest got started for them. This could be in the preface or in the first paragraphs of the introduction to chapter one. Understandably, some students feel uncomfortable "opening up" like that, and there are equally understandable critiques from professors who believe that such first-person anecdotes are irrelevant to the dissertation. Your experiences or perspectives should not be positioned as if you are setting out to prove what you already believed. This is called confirmation bias and is exactly what your theoretical framework and research design were meant to help you avoid. Rather, I believe such experiences are legitimate points of departure for your inquiry and research. They demonstrate why you undertook this research in the first place and may shed light on the importance of your research, giving your committee members a nice starting point to think about your research.

## Formatting the Dissertation

One thing you will have to do—either prior to or right after the defense—is format your dissertation. This means that you have to make your dissertation look basically like every other dissertation out there. This means everything from the headings you use to the format of your charts to the font type and size. While every institution has their own specific standards, most dissertations in the field of education follow APA guidelines or some derivation of it. It is beneficial to format as much of the dissertation up front as possible: for example, use reference software (such as EndNote or RefWorks), create an automated table of contents, and set up your margins correctly from the very first draft. The more you have to redo later on, the larger the problems that could occur. It is completely legitimate to hire a professional editor at this stage of the process. No one can be expected to be an expert on APA style in every single minutia, unless, of course, that is his job. In either case, once formatted, your dissertation will almost surely go through some kind of internal review at your institution. I use the following checklist to make sure that our students' dissertations are formatted appropriately to our standards; it may be helpful to use this or a similar checklist from your own institution to make sure that you have formatted everything correctly.

---

**Use This!**  **Key Formatting Guidelines for Final Submission of Dissertation**

1. **Formatting**

    1.1    Margins: 1.5" on left; 1" top, right, bottom
    1.2    Font and size: Times New Roman, 12 point
    1.3    Line spacing: double-spaced, except tables, appendices
    1.4    Paragraphs: indented a half-inch
    1.5    Appropriate headings
    1.6    Appropriate footnotes or endnotes
    1.7    Left alignment of main text
    1.8    No "widows" or "orphans"
    1.9    Appropriate APA style for in-text citations
    1.10   Consistency

2. **Pagination**

    2.1    Signature page and title page do not have page numbers.
    2.2    All other front matter should have Roman numbering (i.e., i, ii, iii, iv, etc.).
    2.3    Numbering of front matter should be centered on the bottom edge of each page.
    2.4    Numbering of main text should have Arabic numbering (i.e., 1, 2, 3, etc.).
    2.5    Numbering of main text should be in the top, right corner of each page.

3. **Front matter in correct style and order**

    3.1    Signature page
    3.2    Title page
    3.3    Copyright page (optional)
    3.4    Abstract: written in third person; 350 words or less
    3.5    Dedication (optional): written in a professional tone
    3.6    Acknowledgments (optional): written in a professional tone
    3.7    Table of contents
    3.8    List of tables and figures (as needed)
    3.9    Other lists (as needed)
    3.10   Preface (optional): written in a professional tone

4. **Supplemental material in correct style and order**

    4.1    Reference list: All in-text citations linked to reference list (and vice-versa).
    4.2    Appendices
    4.3    Biographical sketch/resume (optional)

---

## Citation Style

Students (and even academics) oftentimes bristle at the seemingly inane requirements of different citation styles such as APA. This is especially true when they are at the very final stages of the dissertation. They are grappling with analyzing intricate and complex research questions, trying to draw out implications for educational policy, and positioning their ideas within a major academic discussion; and I, the dissertation chair, have to tell them to make sure the comma goes inside the quotation mark rather than outside of it. Huh?

There is a logical and rational answer to some of this incredulity. Every specific formatting procedure (whether it is MLA, APA, etc.) is built to support the easy, accurate, and consistent appraisal of data. There would be aesthetic chaos if, for example, you changed the format of each chart in your dissertation. If, moreover, every other academic decided to do their charts in their own idiosyncratic manner, there would be discipline-wide confusion. Likewise, if I wanted to look up one of your references, it would be next to impossible if you did not include—each and every time—key information such as the name of the journal, the volume and issue it was in, and the specific page numbers. An all-encompassing formatting protocol is thus for the benefit of the academic field and not specifically for you the individual. You just have to accept that.

Additionally, no matter how much we may want to ignore it, first impressions matter. If the reader is used to seeing every other academic book and article in APA format, it comes as something of a shock if there is a deviation from this format. The reader will begin to ask some internal questions: Did the author not know this was required in APA format? Did he not care? Did he edit it so quickly that there are other, perhaps larger, errors in the manuscript as well? What does this say about the thoroughness of the data analysis? There may be absolutely no basis for these questions, and the rest of the dissertation could be absolutely top-notch. But the simple and seemingly minor errors in formatting nevertheless raise the reader's suspicions, and he becomes a much more careful and skeptical reader. The effort and energy to abide by formatting standards is thus well spent, allowing the reader to focus on the content of the dissertation rather than on the districting elements that can then seep into the overall impression.

## Chapter Length

You would think that at the dissertation stage, when doctoral students are about to reach the pinnacle of academic accomplishment, they would have stopped asking this question. Yet, I hear it again and again: how long should each chapter be? On one hand, I tell my students, I refuse to answer such a question because it is conceptually incoherent; you should write until you are finished writing what you wanted and needed to say. Nevertheless, I acknowledge the pragmatic necessity of such a question, and while there is no definitive standard, there are some rules of thumb, as outlined below in Figure 6.4.

**Figure 6.4**  Chapter Lengths at Different Stages

|  | Proposal | Dissertation | Post-Dissertation |
|---|---|---|---|
| Chapter One | 20% | 5% | 10% |
| Chapter Two | 40% | 30% | 10% |
| Chapter Three | 40% | 30% | 10% |
| Chapter Four | 0% | 30% | 20% |
| Chapter Five | 0% | 5% | 50% |

*Note:* Percentages are approximations and are articulated as a percentage of the total length of the dissertation. For example, the first chapter should be about 5 percent of the total length of the final dissertation.

At the proposal stage, your committee is looking for the key data in chapters two and three, which should make up the vast majority of the proposal. At the dissertation stage, the literature review, methodology, and findings are all more or less equally important and should all be emphasized and written about at length. Another way to view this is that chapters one and five should be no more than 10 to 15 percent of the overall dissertation. Your committee is much more interested in your mastery of academic protocols—doing a thorough literature review, having a tight and focused methodology, and being able to carefully present and analyze your data—than they are with the big-picture implications. Such implications may be enjoyable and fruitful to talk about at the dissertation defense, but they should not be the central focus of the actual written dissertation.

Interestingly, these big-picture issues become much more relevant in your "post-dissertation" life, which is discussed in the concluding chapter. For now, it may be useful to note that whereas your introduction and conclusion may take up 10 to 15 percent of your dissertation, these ideas should make up the majority of your nonacademic writing. In other words, most general-audience readers are much more interested in the story and the implications than with whether you used a 4-point or 5-point Likert scale in your surveys. Most general-audience readers will actually not even be attuned to the importance of a literature review or a methodology. While you should include a little bit about such points, the heart of your nonacademic writing is really about your findings and the implications that come from them.

Finally, percentages, rather than actual page lengths, should be your reference point because it does not matter if your dissertation is 100 pages or 400 pages. What matters is the proportionality of chapters to each other and to the overall length of the dissertation. But, since doctoral students always ask, we can for the sake of argument assume that a typical dissertation is 150 pages long; as such, chapter one would be between five and fifteen pages; chapters two, three, and four would each be between thirty and fifty pages; and chapter five would be between five and fifteen pages. As usual, there will be exceptions and variations across research methods, writing style, and depth of data. This at least offers some parameters.

## Front Matter

When you are finally, finally, finished with your dissertation draft you are, unfortunately, not quite done. There is still something called the "front matter" or "preliminary pages" that have to be created. The front matter is everything that comes before the actual text: the signature page, title page, copyright page, abstract, dedication, acknowledgements, table of contents, list of tables and figures, and preface. Your institution should have a very

---

### Hint! How to Write a Good Abstract

At a simple level, the abstract is a summary of your dissertation. Usually, you would write the abstract after the dissertation defense, as you can then clearly and accurately summarize your research and findings. At a deeper level, the abstract should be viewed as the most public aspect of your dissertation. The abstract will be the first thing that individuals read and, as such, decide whether to continue reading. It is also what is most accessed by search engines and researchers conducting their own literature reviews. The abstract should thus clearly and succinctly articulate your work. Finally, and building on this last point, the abstract is a synthesis and crystallization of the key components of the dissertation. In other words, a synthesis is not a summary. Your literature review was probably a lot longer than your conclusions; yet, the abstract does not summarize the literature review. It synthesizes your findings. It is thus really difficult to write a good abstract because you must have the necessary "critical distance" to really see what it is you have accomplished.

On a technical level, the abstract should be (1) less than 350 words, (2) singled-spaced as a single paragraph (i.e., don't have paragraph breaks), (3) written in third person, and (4) free of quotes and in-text citations that take up the preciously limited word count.

On a conceptual level, the abstract should (1) focus on the big picture (chapter one), the findings (chapter 4), and the implications (chapter 5); (2) minimally summarize the literature review and methodology; (3) use sequencing (e.g., first . . . second . . . third . . .) to clearly delineate and outline key points and findings; and (4) only refer to the key findings, since the nuances of theoretical frameworks, scholarly debates, and methodological procedures should be left for the actual dissertation.

Finally, ask an "outsider" such as a friend or your advisor for help to make sure that what you have written is clear and sensible. It is very hard to really see something clearly when you have been so close to it for so long.

standardized format for how most of this should be structured. The title page, for example, is a highly standardized page with a formulaic statement that includes your name, the title of your dissertation, and a phrase about this dissertation as being a partial submission for the doctoral degree. Likewise, an abstract has a standard format, which includes being written in the third person, being limited to 350 words or less, and written as one, single-spaced paragraph.

It may be tempting to complete these sections quickly and hurriedly. Don't. First of all, the front matter is literally what every reader sees first. You don't want someone to open your dissertation and immediately see an error or inaccurate formatting. More importantly, the front matter is where you actually have the chance to talk in your own voice. Since the front matter is usually written after the dissertation defense, your committee may not see it until you send them a copy of the final, bound dissertation. As such, it is here where you can thank and acknowledge the people who have helped you along the way. It is here where you can give the reader a sense of your situation without it affecting how the committee looked at the dissertation. Take a little time to reflect on this opportunity. There are probably many, many people who could and should be thanked. And it would be a great sorrow if your hurriedness at this final stage meant that someone important was left out of the acknowledgements.

So now, truly, that's it. You have a final dissertation draft. All that is left is to do is defend it.

# 7

## *Defending and Moving On*

**P**erhaps it is an apocryphal story: doctoral candidates in the Middle Ages would wander from town to town in their long robes and hoods—what has come to be referred to as our "academic regalia"—"defending" their dissertation ideas in front of less-than-civil audiences who might actually throw foodstuff as a sign of their displeasure. From this historical context, so the story goes, the dissertation defense can be a grueling and uncertain event.

Don't be fooled. While my students never believe me, I always say that the dissertation defense can be an incredibly enjoyable experience. As mentioned earlier, it may be one of the very few times that you get to sit down and talk to a few people who have actually carefully read and thought about every aspect of your dissertation. You have probably had innumerable discussions with friends and colleagues about your dissertation: you have told them what it was about, perhaps talked about the difficulties along the way, maybe even shared a few key insights or findings. But most likely, you have never had the opportunity to discuss in detail every major and minor facet of our study. This is your chance. See this as an incredibly wonderful gift that your committee is giving to you: the opportunity to discuss your obsession in detail.

Part of the reason I am being somewhat flippant about the seriousness of the dissertation defense is because I believe in the dissertation process. Put otherwise, you would not be defending your dissertation if your advisor did not believe you were ready to defend and pass. This is not to say you should relax or take it easy and not prepare. It is to say that your advisor is the best judge of when you are ready to defend. You may think it needs two more revisions, or perhaps you thought it was ready two revisions ago. Regardless, when your advisor tells you to send your final draft to your committee, it means she believes you are ready. The question now is, ready for what?

To take a slightly longer view, it becomes necessary to ask a more existential follow-up question: what happens if/when you pass? As already indicated, the dissertation defense is really the first step in the rest of your life as a practitioner scholar. Most of us don't really realize what it means to be a "doctor" until many years after the actual defense. Are we supposed to feel differently? Act differently? Does a doctorate open new and unexpected doors for our careers? Moreover, just like with any life-altering experience, the "post-dissertation" experience is akin to the postpartum blues. There is oftentimes a gaping hole and grief mixed in with the joy of completion. This chapter, as such, walks through the pragmatic and big-picture points of the dissertation defense and what happens afterward. The "afterward" part is a particular focus here, because this is, finally, when your life as a practitioner scholar actually does begin to resemble a journey. A dissertation—as I hope you by now understand—is a highly structured process. Your life, though, isn't. It is thus important to understand what you will have accomplished upon the successful defense of your dissertation. This will give you a vision of what your life journey can actually gain from this experience.

## THE DISSERTATION DEFENSE

Pragmatically, a dissertation defense lasts between one and two hours. Some are open to the public, while others will only include your dissertation committee and perhaps an administrator or faculty representing the school of education or graduate program. Ask your advisor about the specific protocol at your institution, since sometimes the doctoral student can decide on this structure. Usually, even if it is open to the public, only the dissertation committee can talk and ask questions since they are the only ones who have read your dissertation.

You will most likely be asked to give a short summary of your dissertation at the start of the defense, whereupon there will be an open discussion between you and your committee. Keep the summary brief—under ten minutes—since, obviously, your committee has read the dissertation and is much more interested to ask questions and have a discussion. The

**Hint! Key Points About Your Dissertation Defense**

- **Prepare a summary.** You should read or speak for no more than ten to fifteen minutes in your introductory comments. Keep this short, as the real part of the dissertation defense is the discussion.

- **Don't use PowerPoint or other materials.** Your dissertation defense is about your dissertation. There is no need for handouts, slides, or Web-based presentations. Think of it as a discussion. Don't get distracted, and don't distract others, with seemingly fancy gadgets or presentation techniques.

- **Only bring your dissertation draft.** Make sure that you bring the dissertation draft that you sent to your committee. Don't modify anything else in this manuscript, since the committee may want to refer to particular pages and tables. Don't bring supporting materials, raw data, or the books and articles you cited. If you're going to quote anything, do so from your dissertation. Think of the defense as a self-contained event with no need for such external props.

- **Don't get defensive.** Your committee is there to help you (although see the points below about difficult defenses). When they question or critique, it's really for your own benefit as, ideally, they are helping you see your own blind spots and errors in order to make the dissertation better.

- **Be specific.** Refer to page numbers, methodological protocol, and key references in your defense. You want to show your committee that you know your stuff. Don't be vague.

- **Be gracious.** Your committee has invested time and energy into reading and commenting on your dissertation. Even if you don't agree with specific points, write them down.

- **Listen to your dissertation chair.** Whatever she tells you to do after the defense, do it. Don't do more, and don't do less. Your defense is the culminating moment for her as well. She wants you to succeed, and as such, listen to her advice.

- **Have fun.** The dissertation defense is what you have been building toward for long months and years. While it may be new to you, most of your committee has probably sat through many defenses. They probably aren't uptight at all. You don't have to be either. While you don't have to crack jokes, it is okay to see this as an enjoyable event.

- **Remember, it's just a dissertation.** You are not receiving a Noble Prize; your study has limitations; it hasn't solved the world's problems. You have, of course, done a good job and potentially even made an impact on a particular topic. But there is always more to do. Acknowledge that and see this event in its larger context.

summary is an opportunity for you to set the stage, lay out the big-picture issues, provide a synopsis of your findings, and perhaps expand or highlight a specific and noteworthy methodological or theoretical point. A summary is also your chance to clarify any modifications or problems encountered during the data collection or analysis.

The questions from your committee can then be about anything in the dissertation—large or small—and even outside of it. In general, questions and discussion fall into four categories: (1) general clarification, (2) methodological clarification, (3) alignment of data with conclusions, and (4) expansion and next steps. The first type of questioning is benign and helpful for both you and the committee: committee members may not have understood a specific part of your study or its context and may ask you to clarify that. They may also feel that you need to expand something to allow the reader a better understanding of it.

The methodological questions can be the hardest and most important ones of the entire defense. Remember that you have been living with your dissertation for many, many months, whereas your committee may not have heard from you or read anything since you submitted your dissertation proposal long ago. If you actually did look back on your proposal, you would realize just how massively your study has changed. This is completely normal, as the day-to-day reality of data collection, analysis, and writing can never be predicted. You know this. But this may be the first time that your committee has now seen such modifications. So, they have to process these modifications. They are rightly curious and perhaps even skeptical. Ideally, your write-up in chapter three should have explained all of these changes and modifications. But even then, committee members want to probe to ensure that you do in fact understand what you did, how you did it, and the implications and consequences of your methodological procedures.

The key here is exactly the same as it was when you were first fashioning and writing about your research design: clarity and acknowledgment of limitations. The best way to answer methodological questions is to be precise about what you did, how you did it, and why you did what you did. If your committee members find flaws in your design—and they oftentimes do—this does not mean there is a fundamental flaw. Usually, it simply means that they have just provided you with a clearer understanding of the limitations of your study. One of my doctoral students, for example, did a districtwide study of afterschool programs and surveyed all of the programs' leaders and teachers. It became apparent in the defense, though, that the responses to the surveys disproportionately came from programs in a wealthier part of the district. Her findings, the committee thus advised her, may not have been applicable across the entire district. This did not invalidate her study. It simply clarified that her findings were relevant to specific programs in the district, which in turn shed further light on other findings in her study.

Beyond the methodological questioning, the committee will be clearly concerned about whether your conclusions align with your gathered data. Oftentimes, the final chapter of a dissertation is the place where doctoral students finally use their own "voice" and see it as an opportunity to finally give their opinion on the issue. But, their opinion may not match what they found. This is at the crux of being a researcher: your findings may not match your beliefs, other research, or your own highly held hopes. You, though, have to report them. When your dissertation is done, you can do whatever you want with the data and conclusions and your own opinions. In the dissertation, though, the conclusions have to be faithful with the gathered data.

Your committee may go step-by-step asking you about how particular data support particular conclusions, or, alternatively, they may ask you to point out where particular conclusions are supported by the data. This does not, by the way, mean that you should bring your raw data to the defense. Don't show up to the defense with binders and binders of data and articles and journals. The defense is not the place for that. Your advisor should have gone through this stage with you, making sure that the raw data match your analysis and your conclusions. The committee simply wants to look at the next level of analysis. If they find problems, you may indeed have to revisit your raw data. But the defense is not about that.

Finally, your committee will want to discuss the implications of your dissertation. This goes back to the "so what?" and "who cares?" questions at the very beginning. What can you do with these findings? To whom does it matter? How can it be implemented? By whom? It is here that your committee may be of most help to you. Your committee is composed of experts in their respective fields, and many of them may have years and years of practical experience with exactly the issues you have been researching. Take their ideas and advice seriously, for they may have a completely unexpected perspective on the value of your study, and one that you may not have thought about. I remember being asked by the editor of the *Teachers College Record Journal* to provide a sentence from an article I was about to have published that they could use as a highlighted summary. I e-mailed back two or three suggestions; he, though, chose a completely different sentence from my article which, upon reflection, I realized was exactly right in synthesizing my goals for the article. I had just been too close to my work and unable to see the bigger picture.

The presumption so far has been that your dissertation committee is all-wise and all-helpful. This may not be the case. You may feel that their comments and questions are unhelpful or silly. "Did they even read my dissertation?" you may be asking yourself. The dissertation defense, though, is not the place to question or critique your committee. Be gracious. The committee has (ideally) spent a fair amount of time reading and thinking about your work. They have shown up and lent their names to your dissertation. This is, realistically, as much as you can ask from them. Write down their comments and accept that perhaps it is you who does not understand their insightful points rather than the other way around. You can, of course, ask them to clarify or expand upon their points in the defense, or you can always follow-up with questions after the defense is complete if you are truly interested in doing so. But, remember, the defense is yours, not theirs.

The committee's comments and questions, though, may be difficult and uncomfortable ones. Perhaps there are indeed major problems and conflicts that you may or may not have been aware of, and these now come bubbling and exploding out of the woodwork. First, don't be too surprised. It is, in fact, the committee's job to probe and test the limits and assumptions of your dissertation. Many faculty members may also feel that they are actually doing you a disservice if they do not attack or question your positions and arguments. The academy, after all, is all about critique and debate.

Second, realize that these conflicts and issues may have been around long before you came along; your dissertation defense may simply be the occasion within which some faculty continue their long-running disagreements about methodology or theory or educational policy. While it's strange to say this about your own dissertation defense, it really may not be about you.

Finally, you should realize that you cannot "control" or predict your dissertation defense. The defense will have a different combination of questions depending on your committee, your dissertation, etc. It may take a completely unanticipated turn, or probe what you had initially considered a very minor point in the overall dissertation. Assuming that the questioning or seemingly tangential discussion is not moving toward any cataclysmic problem, my recommendation is to "go with the flow."

The bigger part of this advice is that you are now—right there and then—a part of that "community of scholars" spoken about in the first chapter. You are being treated as an equal, an educational scholar who is sitting around a table with other educational scholars, discussing and probing a complicated and important issue with no simple solution. You have a voice at the table, and others are asking for you to make your voice heard. This is a momentous and difficult transition to make. One moment you were a doctoral student following each and every decision of your dissertation chair. The next moment he is asking for your opinion. Accept it and enjoy it. Just like with each stage in your dissertation process, this is one of those unidirectional moments where you cannot go back. You are now an educational scholar with (as they say at the hooding ceremony) all of the privileges and responsibilities thereof. Congratulations.

At some point, of course, the actual dissertation defense will end. Your dissertation chair will ask you and any audience members to step out of the room such that the committee can make a decision. This is basically a pass/fail decision with, if it is a "pass" decision, suggestions and expectations for revisions. And that's it. Really. I got in my car and drove home after my dissertation defense. My wife and I went out to a fancy lunch after her defense. There is unfortunately no momentous rite of passage with trumpets blaring and choirs singing. You are now officially—after the necessary revisions, filing of paperwork, binding of the dissertation, etc.—a doctor.

So, what do you do now? There is no definitive answer to what you should do after your dissertation defense. Unlike the dissertation process, your life is truly unique to you. Some people do nothing with their dissertations. They don't think about it, write about it, or look at it ever again. Some, on the other hand, see the dissertation as a daily and transformative part of their professional lives. One of the doctoral students in our program, for example, was the deputy chief of the educational system in Barbados and used her dissertation as the basis for modifying the entire model of principal preparation and mentoring in her country.

Your experience through the dissertation process may actually have many benefits and implications that you may not be aware of now or know what to do with. Just like with the dissertation, there are

## Hint! How to Handle Conflict and Difficult Situations at Your Dissertation Defense

There is no single or simple way to get out of trouble at a dissertation defense. Hopefully, a difficult situation will not occur at your defense, but there are several measures and steps you can take to minimize any potential problems.

- **Be prepared.** Talk to your chair and committee members before the dissertation defense. Ask them if they foresee any major problems. Ask them, if appropriate, what kinds of questions and critiques you might expect.

- **Determine whether the conflict is really about you.** Oftentimes, the conflict is really between faculty members and has little to do with your dissertation. See if other committee members can come to your defense or offer an alternative perspective on the problem. This can be as simple as asking another committee member whether they have the same concerns. If the problem is truly about something else—such as a theoretical or policy disagreement—acknowledge that your dissertation is not really going to solve this long-standing issue.

- **Try to remember that you do in fact know a lot.** You may not know the most in the room about this issue, though many times, you do. Either way, you do know enough that you should feel comfortable enough to disagree with the critique. It's okay, in fact, to push back and question the validity of their critique and/or the assumptions of their arguments. This may not be pretty, but it's legitimate.

- **Cite, cite, cite.** One of your best defenses is what is actually already written in your dissertation. Cite your sources, cite your data, and, if necessary, cite your dissertation chair. Make clear that your dissertation is simply following the footsteps of many other scholars. If the committee has an issue with your particular argument or stance, then it is questioning an entire body of educational research.

- **Turn the attack into a "limitation."** An attack can be thought about as simply the flip side of a clarification, identifying a limitation of your study. As such, acknowledge the attack and rephrase it positively as a limitation that should indeed be mentioned in the study.

- **Propose that this is "a great follow-up research project."** All dissertations are limited by time, funding, and space. The critique may serve as the impetus to the next analysis of this issue. Clarify that such a "next step" could not have been possible without your own dissertation and your committee member's "insightful" clarification through his criticism.

- **Look to your dissertation chair for support.** Your dissertation chair should be your biggest advocate. What happens to your dissertation is a fundamental reflection on his ability to adequately guide and support you. If you fail, he fails. As such, make sure your dissertation chair gets involved in clarifying or reframing the issue in order to support your arguments and data.

specific heuristics you should take into account as a direct consequence of completing your dissertation. The short and simple consequence is that you must now learn what it means to be a practitioner
scholar. The longer consequence, discussed subsequently, relates to
three distinctive components: publish your findings, apply your
research, and teach the next generation.

## PUBLISH YOUR FINDINGS

All too often, a dissertation becomes nothing more than another book on
your bookshelf and an entry in the immense online dissertation depository
serviced by ProQuest UMI. In fact, the vast majority of dissertations are
never republished in any shape or form. This is not only a shame; it is a disservice. You have spent an enormous amount of time learning about and
researching key data, writings, and benchmarks relevant for your specific
issue. Your findings, hopefully, are meaningful, relevant, and important for
the academic and/or local community. Dozens, if not hundreds, of individuals have supported your work, either by doing interviews, taking surveys,
being observed, or giving you the time and ability to complete this important goal in your career. You yourself have invested years of your life and
tens of thousands of dollars. So, what's stopping you from making your
findings known to a larger audience? The usual answer is a combination of
not knowing where, how, or why you should publish/talk about your findings. In other words, just like the rest of the dissertation process, what to do
afterward with one's findings is all too often shrouded in silence.

The first step is to realize that what you have accomplished in your dissertation matters. It is not trivial, else your dissertation committee would
not have approved it in the first place or allowed it to be successfully
defended. The problem is that you have spent so much time with your
research that it seems both obvious and somehow irrelevant by now. Think
about it: if you heard someone else talking about the same thing for eighteen months day in and day out, you'd probably get tired of hearing about
the issue very quickly. And, the only other people (besides yourself) who
have heard about your dissertation are the professors on your committee,
who either have also heard about it enough by now or are too busy to pay
much attention after the conclusion of the defense. In other words, you
and the few people around you have become inured to the relevance and
potential impact of your dissertation research and findings. Thus, realize
that your dissertation matters to lots of other people outside of yourself
and your committee.

The second step is to start thinking about exactly who that audience
might be. The "traditional" academic answer is other academics, specifically academics in the particular subfield you researched and worked
within. But that's not the whole answer. Your research, in fact, may be

applicable to a huge range of audiences as long as you are able to frame your research and findings to their particular needs. What you need to realize is that there are multiple audiences and multiple means by which to reach such audiences.

Figure 7.1 provides a spectrum of options to potentially disseminate your findings. As you examine these diverse options, it is critical that you are not trapped by the seeming legitimacy of only the academic options on the left-hand side of this spectrum. Since you have been working in the academic sphere for so many months, you have probably become used to and socialized by the need to cite sources, only trust peer-reviewed publications, and be respectful of "what the research says." This is all indeed true. But, it is only true at the dissertation stage, and if you continue to write only for academic audiences. Academics—including those on your dissertation committee—rely on the power and authority of the peer-review system and the long scholarly strands of dialogue, debate, and data that build up over the years on particular educational issues. This is what you worked within, cited, and wrote about in your dissertation in general, and probably in the literature review in chapter two in specific. You may want to continue to write for such an audience. But you also may not.

Newspaper columns or editorials, for example, are read by many more people than a peer-reviewed article. Workshops for teachers or parents can have a profound and immediate impact. Presentations to the superintendent, the school board committee, or to a parent–teacher association meeting can inform policy and decision making at a school or an entire district. These are just a few ideas, for there are numerous ways to write about and present your research and findings, and these may be applicable to and impactful for a wide variety of constituencies. I belong

**Figure 7.1**  Disseminating Your Findings

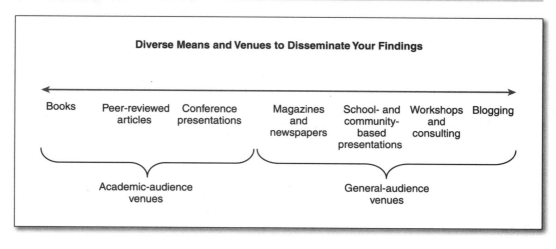

to a group blog that regularly has more readers in one week than many of my academic articles have had in the decade (or so) since they have been published. Because blogging (or newspapers or workshops) can be published or presented in real time or within a week, you can get feedback, a dialogue, or results very, very quickly. That's powerful.

The final step in thinking about disseminating your work is to realize that it is about the quality of venue in which you present/publish your dissertation research and findings. Put otherwise, each type of venue is itself a spectrum. If you want to publish an academic book or peer-reviewed article, for example, it is critical to realize that some presses and journals are much more selective than others. Journal editors call this the "rejection rate." Top academic educational journals, for example, have an 80 to 90 percent rejection rate. The *Review of Educational Research,* the *American Educational Research Journal,* and *Teachers College Record* all have about a 10 percent acceptance rate. Other excellent academic journals (such as *Educational Psychologist* or *Educational Studies*) have an acceptance rate around 30 or 40 percent. A good rule of thumb is that a good academic journal can have anywhere between a 50 to 90 percent rejection rate. This does not mean you shouldn't try to publish in such journals. It simply means that you have to be very deliberate about which journal you choose to submit your work to and that your submission must be high quality.

## Hint! Tips For Academic Journal Publishing

- **Collaborate.** See if one of your committee members is interested in coauthoring an academic article with you. Academic publishing—as any other field—has its myriad of informal and formal rules and norms. It is immensely helpful if someone who has already published can serve as a guide through what can oftentimes feel like a byzantine process. If you do end up collaborating, keep in mind that you are now both "coauthors" and that, traditionally, the individual who does the most work (and has collected the data) is the "first author." It is best to work this out with your collaborator up front so there is no misunderstanding later on.

- **Use your reference list.** The best place to figure out where to publish your research is to see where the authors you have cited have published their own research. Scan through your reference list and see which journals are cited often. These journals are probably the most selective (i.e., they have a high rejection rate), but they may also be the best fit for your findings.

- **Be a part of the conversation.** If at all possible, reference and discuss previous articles in the journal you are interested in publishing in. Journal editors publish articles that they find fascinating, important, and provocative to their particular fields. Journal editors are in many ways the informal stewards of a field.

They want to support specific dialogues and debates. If you can show that you are part of that dialogue, you'll have a much better chance of being published.

- **Follow journal guidelines.** All journals have specific guidelines about length, reference style, etc. Follow them. If the journal uses APA, make sure your document is formatted to APA. If you are not sure what a specific style looks like (e.g., Chicago), simply look at any article published in that journal and mimic their pattern of in-text citations, reference list, etc.

- **Realize that journal editors have very little time.** Most journal editors do the vast majority of the work of publishing a journal; this means everything from soliciting manuscripts, to doing an initial reading of the manuscript, to finding reviewers and synthesizing their comments, to corresponding with authors about accepted and rejected manuscripts, etc. They are busy people. Be mindful of this. When you submit your manuscript, make sure that everything is formatted correctly. Make sure your "cover letter" in your e-mail is brief and to the point. Don't take it personally if they don't respond immediately.

- **Don't worry if you are rejected.** There are two types of "rejection": a "revise and resubmit" and a standard rejection. It is actually a very good sign if a journal editor asks you to revise and resubmit your manuscript. This shows interest in your manuscript if the proper changes can be made. As such, make the changes asked for or be clear about why specific changes are not relevant or reasonable (which is a completely legitimate thing to argue). If you are simply rejected, do what all good academics do: analyze the reasons given for the rejection, make any modifications that seem warranted, and send the manuscript off to the next journal on your list.

- **Understand academic "etiquette" and terminology.**
  - What you have submitted is a "manuscript," not an "article." It becomes an article when it has been accepted for publication. Refer, as such, to it as a manuscript in your e-mail cover letter and in other places (such as your CV), else you may appear presumptuous.
  - When you have submitted your manuscript to a journal, it is "under review." If it is accepted, you can refer to it as an article that is "forthcoming." Once you know which journal issue your article will appear (this can take anywhere from three months to a year), it becomes "in press."
  - Don't submit the manuscript anywhere else while it is under review. If you haven't heard from the editor in a reasonable time (two to three months), it is acceptable to send an e-mail inquiring about the status of your submission.

- **Remember that it's a small world.** The academic world is really very small once you begin to break it down by subfields. Most subfields only have a few hundred "members"; that is, researchers and educators who write about such issues go to the same conferences and publish in and read the same journals. As such, be mindful to be polite and professional in your correspondences and interactions. Academics, like elephants, have long memories.

There is one other thing to be aware of when considering academic publishing: the time to publication. Traditional academic publishing (i.e., journals and books) is slow—very, very slow. It usually takes anywhere from two to six months for a journal to do a first review of your manuscript submission. If your manuscript is accepted, it can then take anywhere from six to twelve months before your article actually gets published. It is thus very common for one to two years to elapse between the time you put the finishing touches on your original manuscript and sent it off for review and when it actually sees the light of day. It is similar with book publishing.

This is an inordinately long time in the educational world, though it is more or less standard practice in the academic world. Many scholars have moved to Web-based journals and other outlets for distributing their findings, but even so, the time to publication can be many months. It is thus important to think about why and for whom you are publishing your findings. If it is for other academics who may be reading your materials in a year or ten years in order to better understand a specific issue, then academic publishing may be appropriate. But if your audience and goals are local and time-sensitive, you may want to consider more general-audience venues. (And, there is no reason why you can't do both at the same time.)

If you thus disseminate your findings for a general audience, realize that there are different norms and strategies for presenting your work. To put it somewhat simplistically for the moment, academics focus primarily on the data while general audiences focus first on the story. Think about how politicians or companies "sell" their ideas: they find an individual who embodies the issue and who the audience can empathize with. Once the audience is "hooked," it becomes possible to present the details and nuances of the issue. Similarly, you want to lead with an anecdote, quote, or situation that signifies the issue. Look again at Figure 6.4 in Chapter 6 as a reminder of the proportions for different audiences.

Finally, remember that what you take for granted now at the conclusion of your dissertation process is actually cutting edge to general audiences. For educators, your knowledge can be highly valuable: it summarizes key research and best practices, helps them view an issue in a new way, and presents insights from your research and findings that can help them to do their job better. Also, you do not need to only share your own findings. It is just as legitimate to write about or reference other researchers' work, so long, of course, as you cite them appropriately. Just because you and other academics know about a classic study from 1973 doesn't mean that anyone else has ever heard about it. Remember that publishing your research and your area of expertise doesn't have to fit the academic mold of your dissertation process. Becoming a part of a community of scholars presumes that you have the capacity to do such research if you so chose, but there are many other ways to impact educational theory, practice, and policy. It is up to you to determine which ones best fit your goals.

# APPLY YOUR RESEARCH

## IMPACTING K–12 EDUCATION

There is, of course, a more direct and obvious means to impact educational policy and practice: apply your dissertation research directly to your educational context. This is exactly the notion of "translational" research, whereby a researcher takes specific academic findings and applies them directly to on-the-ground practices. While it may be strange to hear, you are actually in an ideal position to make this happen as opposed to most other doctoral graduates and researchers.

Traditionally, applied or translational research is a difficult undertaking, as there are distinct differences that need to be traversed in order to bring scholarship into daily practice. An educational innovation may work great in the lab or at one particular school, but how do you transfer it to a new locale with a different student or teacher population? A new line of research may extend the power of an elementary math curriculum, but how should it be applied in, for example, a diverse, under-resourced school? The divide between theory and practice discussed in the very first chapter haunts educational research exactly because what research finds and what schools implement are all too often two distinctly different things.

Yet, the beauty and power of your specific dissertation process is that these two distinctive components—your on-the-ground perspectives and the academic rigor of your dissertation work—are linked from the very beginning. This is why it is so important, again, to maintain your passion throughout the entire process. The last thing I want is for my doctoral students to come to see the dissertation as yet another academic hoop to jump through. They need to feel that their dissertation research is, however tentatively, directly linked to what they care about as active and engaged educators making a difference in their classrooms and schools.

What you have thus hopefully accomplished with your dissertation is a rigorous, valuable, and fascinating academic study that can also be directly applied to your professional life as an educator. The next step is to figure out how to enact it. On one hand, this may seem highly intimidating. "I should do one more study," you say to yourself, "or read more research literature to get a better grasp of the intricacies I didn't examine in as much depth as I should have, or redo my analysis to look at the problem from another perspective." Sure, I say. Sure. But do that after you have attempted to implement your findings.

A community of scholars will talk about, analyze, and research an issue forever. That is the point of a community of scholars. And when you were deep into your dissertation research, that perspective was a highly comforting one, as it allowed you the freedom to probe and question and think. But once you graduate, you are no longer just a part of that community anymore. You are now also a part of the community of practitioner scholars who have to bring such scholarship into action. Think back to when you entered your doctoral program with overflowing ideas and a passion to change the world. Yet, slowly but surely, the academic culture (and this book) dissuaded you from such a perspective. That is not how scholars think, you were told; that is not what research is about, I said to you. At the time, we were right. But you are no longer in an academic context. As such, it is completely possible, and legitimate, to find again that passion and desire, and link it to your newfound skills, knowledge, and research findings. It is completely possible, and necessary, to rekindle a passion for changing the world even as you now realize that things are much more complicated and nuanced than they may at first have appeared.

The philosopher Paul Ricoeur called such a worldview a "second naiveté" whereby the original loss of meaning is overcome to the extent that we are able to have a "double accounting." We are, in other words, able to hold both the deep-seated belief in something while also aware of the criticisms and contradictions of holding such a seemingly naive perspective in the face of science, reason, and logic. Likewise, it is possible to do good, and to make a difference, and be aware that perhaps research has not demonstrated a statistical significance. We may not clearly or easily clarify how that particular practice is differentiated from or builds upon another one, yet we know that we must move forward. Such moving forward should be done with caution, and reflection, and attunement to possible contradictory and problematic implications. But moving forward with the reform effort or the intervention or the new curriculum should become the default option rather than what one does after another 150-page dissertation.

Put otherwise, move forward with implementing your research ideas and findings and don't let them sit on the shelf gathering dust. The first step may be to publicize your findings in a school or district newsletter. You may want to present your dissertation results at the next parent association or school board meeting. You may have the ability to develop a pilot project whereby you try out the ideas in one classroom, at a workshop, or with one cohort group of students. Embrace these opportunities as a chance to put your ideas into practice. Most of these issues have already been worked through in your dissertation; to put it another way, even if you haven't thought everything through, there are probably few people who have done so more than you. Just like with your dissertation defense, realize that the hard work of doing your dissertation has provided you with a set of skills and particular expertise that most other people may not have. Apply them. To paraphrase the first-century Jewish scholar and rabbi Hillel, if not you, then who? And if not now, then when?

# TEACH THE NEXT GENERATION

## TEACHING IN HIGHER EDUCATION

Many educators believe that a doctorate gives them the ability to teach in higher education. In general, this is true. Colleges and universities usually want instructors who have "terminal degrees," which means a doctorate or (less commonly) a JD. The exception to this is community colleges, which regularly hire instructors with master's degrees. Additionally, many colleges and universities will oftentimes hire someone without a terminal degree if that person has unique skills and experiences, or if they cannot find someone with a terminal degree. This latter scenario is very common in special education, where the number of job openings in higher education is greater than the number of individuals applying for such positions. But, what exactly does it mean to teach in higher education?

Many educators see teaching in higher education as the culminating step in their careers, as it is the "highest" you can go. In some respects, this is true. It is exciting and deeply meaningful to teach future teachers and administrators about your areas of specialization. Your impact can be felt not just by the students in your classroom, but also by the students that your students will teach. There is the potential for exponential impact. But, this is not the whole story. You must first understand how faculty work and how status is organized in higher education (see Figure 7.2 below).

**Figure 7.2**  Types of Faculty Positions in Higher Education

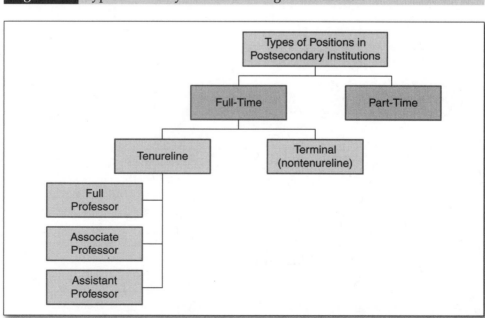

Instructors in higher education (referring here to only four-year institutions) used to be predominantly in full-time tenured or tenure-track positions. This meant that if they received "tenure," which usually occurred after six or seven years at an institution (and is usually denoted by the change in rank from "assistant" to "associate" professor), they would more or less have a secure job for the rest of their academic lives. Tenure—codified and made popular in the first decades of the twentieth century—was seen as a cornerstone of academic freedom because it gave scholars the freedom to pursue their research agendas without the fear of political or partisan retribution. It is this type of professor—slightly disheveled, always in his office or laboratory, lecturing about arcane and controversial topics—that has dominated the cultural and media zeitgeist.

Today, though, this is far from the reality of higher education. In fact, the majority of today's faculty are part-time or in terminal (i.e., nontenure-track) year-to-year positions (Schuster & Finkelstein, 2006). It is beyond the scope of this book to delve into the reasons behind this and the profound implications of this change on higher education over the last twenty years (see, e.g., Bousquet, 2008). Suffice it to say, if your goal is to get a full-time tenure-track position in higher education, it may be harder than you realize. This is not to say that it is not possible. Like any other job, you have to understand how the process works (see the tips below).

### Hint! Tips for Finding a Full-Time Job in Higher Education

- **Where to look.** There are only a few places that advertise for full-time jobs in higher education. Several of the most popular are the *Chronicle of Higher Education* and the Web sites *Inside Higher Ed* and *HigherEdJobs.* Go to these sites before you look in your local newspaper or the human resource department at your local institution.

- **What to look for.** Most of the jobs listed in these places are for full-time positions, and many of these are tenure track. You are most likely looking for jobs listed at the "assistant professor" level. Moreover, most job listings are very specific about what they are looking for: special education, educational leadership, etc. If you don't have experience and expertise in these areas, don't apply.

- **CV versus resume.** K–12 educators (and the rest of the for-profit and nonprofit world) usually talk about resumes. Academics talk about the CV (curriculum vita). Unlike a resume, a CV is supposed to be extensive and focus on your academic background. Therefore, it should include categories and items such as your education (undergraduate through doctoral work), the title of your dissertation, your work experiences, grants applied for and received, and, most important, scholarly work such as conference papers, publications, and service to the profession (such as being a journal reviewer). CVs thus oftentimes run to ten or even twenty pages. Don't be shy and don't summarize. The academy, as you've learned, is a slow and deliberate place. Accept that search committees will be slow and deliberate as well and read your entire CV.

- **What to submit.** When applying for a full-time, tenure-track job, be sure to include all of the key items, which usually include your CV, a cover letter, letters of reference, as well as additional materials such as student evaluations of your previous higher education teaching experiences, sample syllabi from such courses, and a sample of scholarly work. Don't submit materials (such as evaluations and syllabi) from your K–12 career. If you are looking for a full-time position in higher education, the search committee will only want to see documentation of your success in higher education.

- **Expectations.** Full-time faculty are expected to focus on three things in their jobs: teaching, scholarship, and service. Most faculty are expected to teach a broad set of courses that may be out of their areas of expertise; they are expected to keep up with and contribute to the developing knowledge in their fields; and they are expected to "give back" to their academic communities, which can mean a variety of practices ranging from being on and chairing specific committees at their home institution to serving as a reviewer for an academic conference or journal. Additionally, many institutions now expect, or hope, their faculty will apply for grants as a way to generate revenue and enhance prestige.

- **Publish, publish, publish.** One's reputation in higher education is, whether we like it or not, linked to how much you publish and present your work in academic venues. Faculty, of course, get tenure all the time on the strength of their teaching and service to the academic community. However, search committees want to see that you are a good scholar who can convey best practices to their students. They look for candidates who can make names for themselves in their areas of expertise. They want faculty who can bring prestige to the institution, and who can pass the tenure review process. The easiest proxy for all of this is publications.

A full-time, tenure-track job may not be your goal, and perhaps, at this stage, this is not yet clear. I have found that many practitioner scholars are not really interested in having a full-time faculty position so much as having the opportunity to teach college courses as it best fits their schedules. There are actually multiple means by which you can, in a sense, have the best of both worlds: continuing to work in your K–12 capacity as well as participate in higher education.

The most common way to do so is by part-time teaching (or what is oftentimes also called being an "adjunct"). This is not a highly paid position, but it can be an extremely rewarding one. The students are individuals attempting to move up the educational ladder toward the kind of position that you probably have right now. They may be prospective teachers unsure of how to create a lesson plan, second-career changers looking to get into education after a fruitful career elsewhere, or teachers looking to gain their administrative licenses in order to move into the administrative ranks. What you can offer—and what colleges and universities are looking for—is a foot in each world. You have the experience and insights of your K–12 position, and you now know and feel comfortable in the academic-research world. As such, there are a few considerations that may support finding and succeeding in a part-time position in higher education.

First, expect that you would most likely be applying for and teaching introductory, core courses such as educational psychology, educational leadership, or introduction to education. These are oftentimes large courses that all prospective teachers have to take. You would not be expected (or encouraged) to teach your specialization or about your dissertation research; rather, the institution is looking for someone who can teach a standard course in a standard way. It might help to review the department's Web site and course offerings so you can see what is available and what you might be willing and able to teach. You might also want to do a little research on the Web (search for the specific course title and the word "syllabus") to see how other such introductory courses are taught elsewhere; you don't, for example, want to look silly assigning way too many or too few readings, or ones that may not be truly relevant for that kind of course. Doing your "homework" can be a big leg up when the department is looking for candidates, since they are looking for someone who can seemingly walk right into the department, know the course offering, and know how and what to begin teaching.

Second, and in support of this first point, make contact with your local institutions. Small colleges usually have a "department of education" with anywhere from two to twenty faculty, and you can simply contact the department chair; larger colleges and universities have a "school of education," and you probably want to contact the department chair in your area of specialization, whether that is teacher education, educational leadership, special education, or other specific field; large universities usually have "colleges of education" that employ hundreds of full- and part-time professors scattered across a dozen or more departments and programs. Depending on the size and formality of the institution and department, you could just drop by, call, or e-mail your CV and a short letter of introduction expressing your interest in teaching (see the previous tips on differentiating between a CV and a resume). Don't be shy, as most education departments and programs are always looking for adjunct faculty to staff additional sections if enrollment increases or if another part-time faculty member cannot fulfill their teaching obligation.

Finally, realize that there are, in fact, many ways for you to become involved in an education program besides just teaching. Depending on your area of specialization, type of teaching or administrative licensure, and amount of free time, you could in fact be a college supervisor who supervises students in internships or practicum, be an onsite supervising practitioner (a school-based mentor for students in their field-based practicum), or simply make yourself (or your classroom or school) available for guest lectures, guest visits, or even more formal partnerships. Some of these tasks may require formal training or time spent learning the institution's specific protocols and procedures. The big-picture point is that you are a very valuable resource for these education programs exactly because you are able to bridge the K–12 and higher education worlds. Most full-time professors can no longer maintain close connections with schools and classrooms and rely on individuals just like you to support prospective teachers and administrators. The fact that you have an EdD is a key symbol for these education programs that your capacities, knowledge base, and worldview will align with and support their own teaching.

In the end, realize that what you have accomplished as a practitioner scholar in finishing your dissertation and gaining an EdD is very special. You can now offer a unique perspective to future teachers and administrators. Over the years, I have taught an undergraduate Strategies of Teaching course for prospective teachers, and the most enjoyable part of the class is always when I bring in my current doctoral students and graduates to talk to the class. My doctoral students and graduates—current teachers, principals, and supervisors—offer so much to the prospective teachers exactly because they draw on both their experiences in their doctoral program ("Yes, the research says . . .") and link this to their daily lives in the schools. My undergraduates love this, and so do my doctoral students. And, hopefully, so will you.

## THE BEGINNING OF YOUR JOURNEY AS A PRACTITIONER SCHOLAR

So, finally, I suggest that your dissertation is just the beginning. Of course, in one respect, it is an ending, a conclusion to a long and arduous doctoral process. You can point to a bound copy on your bookshelf and state with surety, "Never again." But I want to suggest that it is actually "always again." From your dissertation process, you have gained not a bound copy of a research study. You have gained a new mode of thinking and working. Thus, irrespective of whether or not you ever write or give talks about your research, your research will always be with you. You are now, finally, on your journey as a practitioner scholar.

On one level, you have a much stronger sense of how to do research and of how research is done. When a colleague—be it a teacher or superintendent—suggests that "the research says . . ." X or Y, it is second nature to ask about whether it was qualitative or quantitative research, what the theoretical framework was, how the researcher supported the validity of the study, etc. Upon hearing the answers—if your colleague can even answer such questions—it is second nature as well to wonder aloud whether the researcher thought about disaggregating the data in this way, controlling for that variable, or spent enough time searching for disconfirming cases. You are not now dismissive of educational research. Rather, you have simply become a savvy consumer of it and know its limitations as well as when a study is well done and legitimate.

On another level, such understanding can, in turn, translate on a daily level. One of my doctoral students, an elementary school principal, now sends out Web-based surveys for every occasion—to his teachers, parents, students, and colleagues at other schools. He has taken it upon himself to investigate the raw data that the commissioner of education recently released about patterns of principal leadership styles and implications for classroom practice. He questions his superintendent as to whether the district's data analyses across subpopulations of students are statistically significant. He himself talks about this transformation as living and breathing data-driven decision making since he learned of its relevance and importance.

But beyond the knowledge gained and its daily use, what I see most strikingly in my graduated doctoral students is their implicit relationship to the world. (No, I'm not going to define that for you or operationalize it or attempt to measure it through a Likert scale; that will be my next dissertation. . . .) It is a way I see them talk about and think about issues.

To be bold, I would call it a certain kind of intellectual swagger. But let me back off such bravado to simply suggest that when they are faced with a problem—be it pragmatic or academic—one can almost see the wheels start to turn inside the heads as gears start shifting and cogs start falling into place: Can we analyze it from this perspective or that one? What are the assumptions behind that kind of framing of the problem? What have others done or said about this problem? How can we gather data to test our hypothesis? What would success look like? Is this really just one problem or a nested set of related problems?

I watch that reflection in action as they begin to "chunk" the problem into manageable pieces in order to get a handle on it. What they are doing, even if they wouldn't put it into these exact words, is redoing their dissertations. But instead of their original dissertation topic, they are doing it with a new problem. Instead of twelve or eighteen months, they are doing it in real time. So that "never again" is really not about their dissertations. It is about a certain way of thinking. Never again will they view issues as blobs and never again will they be stymied about where to look for ideas and examples and the research. This is, of course, an exaggeration. Not every doctoral graduate will think or act like this. Even if they did, this does not make them superhuman. There are lots and lots of smart people around doing just fine who have never gone through a doctoral program.

This is also not to say that your journey now is some kind of competition. Now complete, your dissertation process allows you to sail off on a very different kind of journey. The British philosopher Ludwig Wittgenstein had a wonderful metaphor for how language changed the way we view and relate to the world: he suggested that it was like climbing a ladder and with each step, the one below just falls away. Once you are over a certain threshold, you can't go back. It is the same way with the dissertation. There will naturally be many other issues ahead of you, but your success in climbing up this particular one, in this particular way, gives you the tools for the future. Use them well.

# Key Resources by Topic

## GENERAL READINGS ON RESEARCH METHODS AND DESIGN

Becker, H. (1998). *Tricks of the trade.* Chicago: University of Chicago Press.

Bernard, H. R. (1994). *Research methods in anthropology: Qualitative and quantitative approaches* (2nd ed.). Thousand Oaks, CA: Sage.

Creswell, J. W. (2003). *Research design: Qualitative, quantitative, and mixed-methods approaches* (2nd ed.). Thousand Oaks, CA: Sage.

Denzin, N., & Lincoln, Y. (Eds.). (2003). *The landscape of qualitative research: Theories and issues* (2nd ed.). Thousand Oaks, CA: Sage.

Fraenkel, J. R., & Wallen, N. E. (2003). *How to design and evaluate research in education.* New York: McGraw-Hill.

Johnson, R. B., & Christensen, L. B. (2004). *Educational research: Quantitative, qualitative, and mixed approaches.* Boston: Allyn & Bacon.

Merriam, S. B. (1998). *Qualitative research and case study applications in education.* San Francisco: Jossey-Bass.

Miles, M. B., & Huberman, A. M. (1994). *Qualitative data analysis: A sourcebook of new methods.* Thousand Oaks, CA: Sage.

Patton, M. Q. (1990). *Qualitative evaluation and research methods* (2nd ed.). Newbury Park, CA: Sage.

## FOUNDATIONAL READINGS ON
## RESEARCH METHODS AND DESIGN

Berger, P. L., & Luckman, T. (1967). *The social construction of reality.* New York: Doubleday-Anchor.

Biesta, G., & Burbules, N. C. (2003). *Pragmatism and educational research.* Lanham, MD: Rowman & Littlefield.

Clifford, J., & Marcus, G. E. (1986). *Writing culture: The poetics and politics of ethnography.* Berkeley: University of California Press.

Freire, P. (1970). *Pedagogy of the oppressed.* New York: Herder & Herder.

Geertz, C. (1988). *Works and lives: The anthropologist as writer.* Stanford, CA: Stanford University Press.

Giroux, H. (1983). *Theory and resistance in education.* New York: Bergin & Harvey.

Habermas, J. (1996). *The philosophical discourse of modernity: Twelve lectures.* Cambridge: MIT Press.

Harding, S. G. (Ed.). (1987). *Feminism and methodology: Social science issues.* Milton Keynes, Buckinghamshire, UK: Open University Press.

Kuhn, T. (1967). *The structure of scientific revolutions.* Chicago: University of Chicago Press.

Phillips, D. C., & Burbules, N. C. (2000). *Postpositivism and educational research.* New York: Rowman & Littlefield.

## READINGS ON QUALITATIVE-RESEARCH METHODS AND DESIGN

Denzin, N. K. (1989). *Interpretive biography.* Newbury Park, CA: Sage.

Fetterman, D. M. (1989). *Ethnography step-by-step.* Newbury Park, CA: Sage.

Greenwood, D. J., & Levin, M. (2007). *Introduction to action research: Social research for social change* (2nd ed.). Thousand Oaks, CA: Sage.

Jorgensen, D. L. (1989). *Participant observation: A methodology for human studies.* Thousand Oaks, CA: Sage.

Krueger, R. A. (1988). *Focus groups: A practical guide for research.* Newbury Park, CA: Sage.

Mishler, E. G. (1986). *Research interviewing: Context and narrative.* Cambridge, MA: Harvard University Press.

Seidman, I. (1998). *Interviewing as qualitative research: A guide for researchers in education and the social sciences.* New York: Teachers College Press.

Strauss, A., & Corbin, J. (1990). *Basics of qualitative research: Grounded theory procedures and techniques.* Newbury Park, CA: Sage.

Weber, R. P. (1985). *Basic content analysis.* Beverly Hills, CA: Sage.

## READINGS ON QUANTITATIVE-RESEARCH METHODS AND DESIGN

Czaja, R., & Blair, J. (1996). *Designing surveys: A guide to decisions and procedures.* Thousand Oaks, CA: Pine Forge Press.

Levin, I. P. (1999). *Relating statistics and experimental design.* Thousand Oaks, CA: Sage.

Maxwell, S. E., & Delaney, H. D. (2004). *Designing experiments and analyzing data.* Mahwah, NJ: Lawrence Erlbaum.

Shadish, W. R., Cook, T. C., & Campbell, D. T. (2002). *Experimental and quasi-experimental designs for generalized causal inference.* Boston: Houghton-Mifflin.

## READINGS ON MIXED METHODS AND DESIGN

Green, J. C., Caracelli, V. J., & Graham, W. F. (1989). Toward a conceptual framework for mixed-method evaluation designs. *Educational Evaluation and Policy Analysis, 11*(3), 255–274.

Howe, K. R. (1992). Getting over the quantitative-qualitative debate. *American Journal of Education, 100,* 236–256.

Ragin, C. C. (1987). *The comparative method: Moving beyond qualitative and quantitative strategies.* Berkeley: University of California Press.

Tashakkori, A., & Teddlie, C. (Eds.). (2002). *Handbook of mixed methods in social and behavioral research.* Thousand Oaks, CA: Sage.

# References

American Association of University Women (AAUW). (1992). *How schools shortchange girls*. Washington, DC: Author.

Archbald, D. (2008). Research versus problem solving for the education leadership doctoral thesis: Implications for form and function. *Educational Administration Quarterly, 44*(5), 704–739.

Balfanz, R., & Legters, N. (2004). *Locating the dropout crisis*. Baltimore: Johns Hopkins University Press.

Barnett, B., & Muth, T. (2008). Using action-research strategies and cohort structures to ensure research competence for practitioner scholar leaders, *Journal of Research on Leadership Education, 3*(1), 1–42. Retrieved from http://www.ucea.org/JRLE/v013_issue1_2008/BarnettFinal.pdf

Becker, H. (1998). *Tricks of the trade*. Chicago: University of Chicago Press.

Berk, R. (1983). An introduction to sample selection bias in sociological data. *American Sociological Review, 48*, 386–398.

Berliner, D. (2002). Educational research: The hardest science of all. *Educational Researcher, 31*(8), 18–20.

Berliner, D. (2006). Our impoverished view of educational reform. *Teachers College Record, 108*(6), 949–995.

Bolman, L., & Deal, T. (1991). *Reframing organizations: Artistry, choice, and leadership*. San Francisco: Jossey-Bass.

Bourdieu, P., & Passeron, J. C. (1990). *Reproduction in education, society and culture*. Newbury Park, CA: Sage.

Bousquet, M. (2008). *How the university works: Higher education and the low-wage nation*. New York: New York University Press.

Bransford, J., Brown, A. L., & Cocking, R. R. (Eds.). (2000). *How people learn: Brain, mind, experience, and school*. Washington, DC: National Academy Press.

Brewer, J., & Hunter, A. (1989). *Multimethod research: A synthesis of styles*. Newbury Park, CA: Sage.

Bryman, A. (1984). The debate about quantitative and qualitative research: A question of method or epistemology? *British Journal of Sociology, 35*, 78–92.

Burawoy, M. (1991). *Ethnography unbound*. Berkeley: University of California Press.

Burawoy, M. (1998). The extended case method. *Sociological Theory, 16*(1), 4–33.

Chase, W. G., & Simon, H. A. (1973). Perception in chess. *Cognitive Psychology, 1*, 33–81.

Cleary, R. E. (2000). The public administration doctoral dissertation reexamined: An evaluation of the dissertations of 1998. *Public Administration Review, 60*(5), 446–455.

Clifford, G. J., & Guthrie, J. W. (1988). *Ed school: A brief for professional education.* Chicago: University of Chicago Press.

Clifford, G. J., & Marcus, G. E. (1986). *Writing culture: The poetics and politics of ethnography.* Berkeley: University of California Press.

Collins, R. (1988). The micro foundations of macro sociology. *Sociological Theory, 6,* 242–253.

Cook, T. C., & Campbell, D. (1979). *Quasi-experimentation: Design and analysis issues.* Chicago: Rand McNally.

Council on Graduate Schools PhD Completion Project. (2008). *Promising practices: Student selection and admission.* Retrieved from http://www.phdcompletion .org/promising/selection.asp

Creswell, J. W. (2003). *Research design: Qualitative, quantitative, and mixed-methods approaches* (2nd ed.). Thousand Oaks, CA: Sage.

Czaja, R., & Blair, J. (1996). *Designing surveys: A guide to decisions and procedures.* Thousand Oaks, CA: Pine Forge Press.

Deering, T. E. (1998). Eliminating the doctor of education degree: It's the right thing to do. *Educational Forum, 62*(3), 243–248.

de Groot, A. D. (1965). *Thought and choice in chess.* Amsterdam: Mouton Press.

Delpit, L. (1995). *Other's peoples children: Cultural conflict in the classroom.* New York: New Press.

Denzin, N., & Lincoln, Y. (Eds.). (2003). *The landscape of qualitative research: Theories and issues* (2nd ed.). Thousand Oaks, CA: Sage.

Derrida, J. (1976). *Of grammatology.* Baltimore: Johns Hopkins University Press.

Derrida, J. (1978). *Writing and difference.* Chicago: University of Chicago Press.

Dewey, J. (1916). *Democracy and education.* New York: Macmillan.

Di Pierro, M. (2007). Excellence in doctoral education: Defining best practices. *College Student Journal, 41*(2), 368–375.

Duke, D., & Beck, S. (1999). Education should consider alternative formats for the dissertation. *Educational Researcher, 28*(3), 31–36.

Education Trust. (2006). *Yes we can: Telling truths and dispelling myths about race and education in America.* Retrieved from http://www2.edtrust.org/NR/rdonlyres/ DD58DD01-23A4-4B89-9FD8-C11BB072331E/0/YesWeCan.pdf

Fine, M. (1991). *Framing dropouts: Notes on the politics of an urban public high school.* Albany: SUNY Press.

Fish, S. E. (2008). *Save the world on your own time.* New York: Oxford University Press.

Fraenkel, J. R., & Wallen, N. E. (2003). *How to design and evaluate research in education.* New York: McGraw-Hill.

Gardner, S. K. (2008). What's too much and what's too little? The process of becoming an independent researcher in doctoral education. *Journal of Higher Education, 79*(3), 326–350.

Geertz, C. (1973). *Interpretation of culture: Selected essays.* New York: Basic Books.

Geiger, R. (1997). Doctoral education: The short-term crisis vs. long-term challenge. *The Review of Higher Education, 20*(3), 239–251.

Ghezzi, P. (2007). The online doctorate: Flexible, but credible? *School Administrator, 64*(7), 30–35.

Gladwell, M. (2008). Most likely to succeed. *The New Yorker Magazine*, December 12, 2008.

Goenner, C. F., & Snaith, S. S. (2004). Predicting graduation rates: An analysis of student and institutional factors at doctoral universities. *Journal of College Student Retention, 5*(4), 409–420.

Golde, C. M. (2000). Should I stay or should I go? Student descriptions of the doctoral attrition process. *The Review of Higher Education, 23*(2), 199–227.

Golde, C. M. (2005). The role of the department and discipline in doctoral student attrition: Lessons from four departments. *Journal of Higher Education, 76,* 669–700.

Golde, C. M., & Dore, T. M. (2001). *At cross purposes: What the experiences of today's doctoral students reveal about doctoral education.* Philadelphia: Pew Charitable Trusts.

Golde, C. M., & Walker, G. E. (Eds.). (2006). *Envisioning the future of doctoral education: Preparing stewards of the discipline.* San Francisco: Jossey-Bass.

Goldenberg, C. (1992). The limits of expectations: A case for case knowledge about teacher expectancy effects. *American Educational Research Journal, 29*(3), 517–544.

Green, J. C., Caracelli, V. J., & Graham, W. F. (1989). Toward a conceptual framework for mixed-method evaluation designs. *Educational Evaluation and Policy Analysis, 11*(3), 255–274.

Greene, J. P. (2002). *High school graduation rates in the United States.* New York: Manhattan Institute. Retrieved from http://www.manhattan-institute.org/html/cr_baeo.htm

Greenwood, D. J., & Levin, M. (2007). *Introduction to action research: Social research for social change* (2nd ed.). Thousand Oaks, CA: Sage.

Grogan, M., Donaldson, J., & Simmons, J. (2007). Disrupting the status quo: The action research dissertation as a transformative strategy. In NCPEA (Ed.), *The handbook of doctoral programs: Issues and challenges.* Houston, TX: NCPEA. Retrieved from http://cnx.org/content/m14529/latest

Harding, S. G. (Ed.). (1987). *Feminism and methodology: Social science issues.* Buckinghamshire, UK: Open University Press.

Herr, K., & Anderson, G. L. (2005). *The action research dissertation: A guide for students and faculty.* Thousand Oaks, CA: Sage.

Hess, F. M., & Kelly, A. P. (2005). An innovative look, a recalcitrant reality: The politics of principal preparation reform, *Educational Policy, 19*(1), 155–180.

Hodder, I. (2003). The interpretation of documents and material culture. In N. K. Denzin & Y. S. Lincoln (Eds.), *Collecting and interpreting qualitative materials* (2nd ed., pp. 155–175). Thousand Oaks, CA: Sage.

Holbrook, A., Bourke, S., Lovat, T., & Fairbarn, H. (2008). Consistency and inconsistency in PhD thesis examination. *Australian Journal of Education, 52*(1), 36–48.

Holsti, O. R. (1969). *Content analysis for the social sciences and humanities.* Reading, MA: Addison-Wesley.

Howard, G. S., & Dailey, P. R. (1979). Response-shift bias: A source of contamination of self-report measures. *Journal of Applied Psychology, 64*(2), 144–150.

Howe, K. R. (1988). Against the quantitative-qualitative incompatability thesis, or, Dogmas die hard. *Educational Researcher, 17,* 10–16.

Howe, K. R. (1992). Getting over the quantitative-qualitative debate. *American Journal of Education, 100,* 236–256.

Ioannidis, J. (2005). Why most published research findings are false. *PLoS Med,* *2*(8), e124. doi:10.1371/journal.pmed.0020124

Ivankova, N. V., & Stick, S. L. (2007). Student persistence in a distributed doctoral program in educational leadership in higher education. *Research in Higher Education, 48*(1), 93–135.

James, W. (1903, March). The PhD Octopus. *Harvard Monthly.* Retrieved from http://www.des.emory.edu/mfp/octopus.html

Johnson, R. B., & Onwuegbuzie, A. J. (2006). Mixed methods research: A paradigm whose time has come. *Educational Researcher, 33*(7), 14–26.

Kam, B. H. (1997). Style and quality in research supervision: The supervisor dependency factor. *Higher Education, 34*(1), 81–103.

Keeton, M. T., Sheckley, B. G., & Griggs, J. (2002). *Effectiveness and efficiency in higher education for adults: A guide for fostering learning.* Dubuque, IA: Kendell/Hunt Publishing.

Labaree, D. F. (2003). The peculiar problems of preparing educational researchers, *Educational Researcher, 32*(4), 13–22.

Labaree, D. F. (2004). *The trouble with ED schools.* New Haven, CT: Yale University Press.

Levin, H. M. (2006). Can research improve educational leadership? *Educational Researcher, 35*(8), 38–43.

Levine, A. (2005). *Educating school leaders.* Washington, DC: The Education Schools Project.

Levine, A. (2007). *Educating educational researchers.* Washington, DC: The Education Schools Project.

Lincoln, Y. S., & Guba, E. G. (1985). *Naturalistic inquiry.* Beverly Hills, CA: Sage.

Lovitts, B. E. (2001). *Leaving the ivory tower: The causes and consequences of departure from doctoral study.* Lanham, MD: Rowman & Littlefield.

Lovitts, B. E. (2005). How to grade a dissertation. *Academe, 91*(6), 18–23.

Lovitts, B. E., & Nelson, C. (2000). The hidden crisis in graduate education attrition from PhD programs. *Academe, 86,* 44–50.

Malone, B. G., Nelson, J. S., & Nelson, C. V. (2004). Academic and affective factors contributing to degree completion of doctoral students in educational administration. *The Teacher Educator, 40*(1), 33–55.

Martin, M. W., & Sell, J. (1979). The role of the experiment in the social sciences. *Sociological Quarterly, 20,* 581–590.

Maxcy, S. J. (2003). Pragmatic threads in mixed methods research in the social sciences: The search for multiple modes of inquiry and the end of the philosophy of formalism. In A. Tashakkori & C. Teddlie (Eds.), *Handbook on mixed methods in the behavioral and social sciences* (pp. 51–89). Thousand Oaks, CA: Sage.

McWilliam, E., Lawson, A., & Evans, T. (2005). "Silly, soft and otherwise suspect": Doctoral education as risky business. *Australian Journal of Education, 49*(2), 214–227.

Merriam, S. B. (1998). *Qualitative research and case study applications in education.* San Francisco: Jossey-Bass.

Mertens, D. M. (2003). Mixed methods and the politics of human research: The transformative-emancipatory perspective. In A. Tashakkori & C. Teddlie (Eds.), *Handbook of mixed methods in social and behavioral research* (pp. 135–164). Thousand Oaks, CA: Sage.

Mezirow, J. (1981). A critical theory of adult learning and education. *Adult Education Quarterly, 32*(1), 3–24.

Mezirow, J. (1997). Transformative learning: Theory to practice. *New Directions for Adult and Continuing Education, 74,* 5–12.

Miller, J. (2000). The protection of human subjects in street ethnography. *Focaal, 36,* 53–68.

Oakes, J. M. (2002). Risks and wrongs in social science research: An evaluator's guide to the IRB. *Evaluation Review, 26*(5), 443–480.

Ogbu, J. (1970). *Minority education and caste: The American system in cross-cultural perspective.* New York: Academic Press.

Orr, M. T. (2007). The doctoral debate. *School Administrator, 64*(7), 16–17, 19–20.

Osguthorpe, R. T., & Wong, M. J. (1993). The PhD versus the EdD: Time for a decision. *Innovative Higher Education, 18*(1), 47–63.

Planty, M., Hussar, W., Snyder, T., Provasnik, S., Kena, G., Dinkes, R., et al. (2008). *The condition of education 2008.* Washington, DC: National Center for Education Statistics, Institute of Education Sciences, U.S. Department of Education. Retrieved from http://nces.ed.gov/pubsearch/pubsinfo.asp?pubid=2009081

Preis, S., Grogan, M., Sherman, W. H., & Beaty, D. M. (2007). What the research and literature say about the delivery of educational leadership preparation programs in the United States. *Journal of Research on Leadership Education, 2*(2), 1–36. Retrieved from http://www.ucea.org/JRLE/pdf/v012_issue1__2007/Preisetal.pdf

Ragin, C. C. (1987). *The comparative method: Moving beyond qualitative and quantitative strategies.* Berkeley: University of California Press.

Ragin, C. C., & Becker, H. S. (Eds.). (2002). *What is a case? Exploring the foundations of social inquiry.* New York: Cambridge University Press.

Reason, R. D. (2003). Student variables that predict retention: Recent research and new developments. *NASPA Journal, 40*(4), 172–191.

Richardson, R. (2006). Stewards of a field, stewards of an enterprise: The doctorate in education. In C. Golde, G. Walker, & Associates (Eds.), *Envisioning the future of doctoral education: Essays on the doctorate* (pp. 251–267). San Francisco: Jossey-Bass.

Rosen, B. C., & Bates, A. P. (1967). The structure of socialization in graduate school. *Sociological Inquiry, 37,* 71–84.

Rosenthal, R., & Jacobson, L. (2003). *Pygmalion in the classroom.* New York: Crown House Publishing. (Original work published in 1968)

Ryle, G. (1971). The thinking of thoughts. What is "Le Penseur" doing. In *Collected papers* (Vols. 1–2, pp. 480–496). New York: Barnes and Noble.

Sadker, M. & Sadker, D. (1995). *Failing at fairness.* New York: Simon and Schuster.

Schön, D. A. (1983). *The reflective practitioner.* New York: Basic Books.

Schrag, F. (1992). In defense of positivist research paradigms. *Educational Researcher, 21*(5), 5–8.

Schuster, J., & Finkelstein, M. (2006). *The restructuring of academic work and careers: The American faculty.* Baltimore: Johns Hopkins University Press.

Schwarz, N. (1999). Self-reports: How the questions shape the answers. *American Psychologist, 54*(2), 93–105.

Seidman, I. (1998). *Interviewing as qualitative research: A guide for researchers in education and the social sciences.* New York: Teachers College Press.

Senge, P. M. (1996). Leading learning organizations: The bold, the powerful, & the invisible. In M. Goldsmith & F. Hasselbein (Eds.), *The leader of the future* (pp. 41–58). San Francisco: Jossey-Bass.

Sherman, W. H., & Beaty, D. M. (2007). The use of distance technology in leadership preparation. *Journal of Educational Administration, 45*(5), 605–620.

Shields, P. M. (1998). Pragmatism as a philosophy of science: A tool for public administration. In J. White (Ed.), *Research in public administration* (Vol. 4, pp. 195–225). Stamford, CT: JAI Press.

Shields, P. M., & Tajalli, H. (2006). Intermediate theory: The missing link to successful student scholarship. *Journal of Public Affairs Education, 12*(3), 313–334.

Shulman, L. S. (2007). Practical wisdom in the service of professional practice. *Educational Researcher, 36*(9), 560–563.

Shulman, L. S., Golde, C. M., Conklin-Bueschel, A., & Garabedian, K. J. (2006). Reclaiming education's doctorates: A critique and a proposal. *Educational Researcher, 35*(3), 25–32.

Spillett, M. A., & Moisiewicz, K. A. (2004). Cheerleader, coach, counselor, critic: Support and challenge roles of the dissertation advisor. *College Student Journal, 38*(2), 246–256.

Tisdell, E. J. (1998). Poststructural feminist pedagogies: The possibilities and limitations of feminist emancipatory adult learning theory and practice. *Adult Education Quarterly, 48*(3), 139–156.

Weick, K. (1995). *Sensemaking in organizations.* Thousand Oaks, CA: Sage.

White, J. D. (1986). Dissertations and publications in public administration. *Public Administration Review, 46*(3), 227–234.

Winter, R., Griffiths, M., & Green, K. (2000). The "academic" qualities of practice: What are the criteria for a practice-based phd? *Studies in Higher Education, 25*(1), 25–37.

Woodrow Wilson Foundation. (2005). *The responsive PhD.* Princeton, NJ: Woodrow Wilson National Fellowship Foundation. Retrieved from http://www .woodrow.org/images/pdf/resphd/ResponsivePhD_overview.pdf

Young, M. D. (2006). From the director: The M.Ed., Ed.D. and Ph.D. in educational leadership. *UCEA Review, XLV*(2), 6–9.

# *Index*

**CORWIN**

A SAGE Company

The Corwin logo—a raven striding across an open book—represents the union of courage and learning. Corwin is committed to improving education for all learners by publishing books and other professional development resources for those serving the field of PreK–12 education. By providing practical, hands-on materials, Corwin continues to carry out the promise of its motto: **"Helping Educators Do Their Work Better."**